Ms. and the Material Girls

PERCEPTIONS OF WOMEN FROM THE 1970s THROUGH THE 1990s

Catherine Gourley

Twenty-First Century Books • Minneapolis

For the "crones"—

Beth, Felicia, Jean, and Marty—wise women all

Twenty-First Century Books
A division of Lerner Publishing Group, Inc.
241 First Avenue North
Minneapolis, MN 55401 U.S.A.

Website address: www.lernerbooks.com

Library of Congress Cataloging-in-Publication Data

Gourley, Catherine, 1950–
 Ms. and the material girls : perceptions of women from the 1970s through the 1990s / by Catherine Gourley.
  p.cm. — (Images and issues of women in the Twentieth Century)
 Includes bibliographical references and index.
 ISBN 978–0–8225–6806–3 (lib. bdg. : alk. paper)
 1. Women in popular culture—United States—History—20th century. 2. Women in mass media—United States—History—20th century. 3. Feminism—United States—History—20th century. I. Title.
HQ1421.G682008
305.420973'09045—dc22   2006100249

Manufactured in the United States of America
1 2 3 4 5 6 – JR – 13 12 11 10 09 08

Contents

The Women's Strike of August 26, 1970, was a rallying point for feminists — and a turning point in the fight for truly equal rights for women. After fifty years of suffrage, American women still were not politically or economically empowered. They felt the situation had to change.

AUTHOR'S NOTE

With a warning to "be good," my parents dropped me off at the girls' boardinghouse, where I would live for the next three months. The four-story building was a block away from the Atlantic Ocean in the quiet shoreline community of Ocean Grove, New Jersey. How quiet was Ocean Grove? The town was "dry," which meant no alcoholic beverages were allowed. And on Sundays, officials hung a heavy chain across the main entrance to the town to enforce the no-cars-allowed rule. But just a short walk north along the beach was Asbury Park and a boardwalk that was anything but quiet. I couldn't wait for my parents' car to drive out of view. It was 1970, and I was nineteen and a sophomore in college. For the first time ever, I was living on my own with no one to tell me when to come home or what to wear. The two most important things I had brought with me were my guitar and my journal. I felt very grown up.

I did not know then who Elizabeth Cady Stanton was or how she had fought for women's rights. And I had never read what she had written about girls, that she would have them "regard

By the early 1970s, American women were banding together in ever greater numbers to demonstrate and work toward economic, social, and political equality. Their work during that decade led to important legislation, including Title IX (outlawing institutional discrimination), the Equal Pay Act, and the Educational Equity Act. This photo shows a women's liberation demonstration in New York in August 1970.

themselves not as adjectives but as nouns." That summer I thought of myself in adjectives: long hair, wide smile, and terrific suntan. I stared enviously at images in popular magazines such as *Glamour* and thought of those female models in terms of adjectives, too: pretty, flirtatious, and daring.

I didn't earn much money that summer, but I learned important things about the world and about myself. I met my first Vietnam War veteran, a young man just two years older than I with shrapnel scars on his chest. I experienced my first civil rights demonstrations when Asbury Park exploded that summer in what the media called "race riots." I met other young women from across the country and listened to their concerns about equal rights for women. When my parents came back for me just after Labor Day, I had more than a terrific suntan. I had "nouns." Because that summer, I became an antiwar protester, a civil rights demonstrator, and a liberated woman who began to look at those magazine models with a more critical eye.

This book is the fifth and last in a series on women's images and issues in the twentieth century. It begins in 1970 and attempts to answer two key questions: How did the popular media of the 1970s, 1980s, and 1990s portray women? Were those images of women accurate or misleading? Such images can appear in any number of ways, among them advertisements, magazine and newspaper articles, television shows, movies, or even song lyrics.

Throughout the twentieth century, media images—whether fact or fiction, stereotypical or sensationalized—influenced women's perception of themselves. But the influence was not always blind acceptance. The conflicting images of popular culture and the ways women reacted to those images is what this series is all about. As you read, you, too, will travel back in time. I hope you'll return to the world of the twenty-first century with a greater understanding of how popular culture may have influenced your mother or your grandmother. More important, I hope you, too, will acquire "nouns" and not just glossy adjectives.

—*Catherine Gourley*

*t*prologue *he women's strike for equality,*
august 26, 1970

Feminists march in New York City on August 26, 1970.

As a black person, I am no stranger to race prejudice. But the truth is that in the political world I have been far oftener discriminated against because I am a woman than because I am black.

—*Shirley Chisholm, "Equal Rights for Women," May 21, 1969*

No one knew for certain what might happen,

just that something would. The National Organization for Women (NOW) had called for housewives and women who worked outside the home to remove their aprons or put down their secretary's notebooks and walk off the job for a day.

The leaders of NOW had carefully selected the date for their public demonstration. August 26, 1970, marked the fiftieth anniversary of the Nineteenth Amendment to the U.S. Constitution, which gave women the right to vote. A popular 1970 advertising campaign for Virginia Slims cigarettes showed pencil-slim, glamorous women smoking equally pencil-slim and seemingly glamorous cigarettes. The campaign slogan claimed "You've come a long way, baby." But had women really made such great achievements in those fifty years since winning suffrage? NO! said NOW.

In 1963 President Kennedy had signed the Equal Pay Act, making it illegal to pay a woman less than a man for doing the same job. Despite the law, in 1970 women still earned approximately 59 percent of what men earned. In some places of employment, a man with an eighth-grade education could earn more than a woman who had graduated from high school or attended college.

In 1970 approximately 25,000 American women were physicians. There were, however, 300,000 male physicians. One reason for this difference is that most medical schools limited the number of women they would accept to just 5 or 10 percent of each class. The same was true for most law schools. Only about 5 percent of the law degrees in 1970 went to women. Even if a woman did receive a law degree—as did future U.S. Supreme Court associate justice Ruth Bader Ginsburg, graduating first in her class from New York's Columbia Law School—a law firm might not

This 1970s ad for cigarettes shows women wearing designer fashions and smoking cigarettes in public. Yet this was not what feminists of the 1970s thought of as progress. They were seeking true equality under the law.

hire her. Why? Some firms believed that their clients would not accept legal advice from a woman. Sandra Day O'Connor, the first woman to serve on the Supreme Court, graduated in the 1950s at the top of her class from law school too. A Los Angeles, California, law firm offered her a job—as a legal secretary. She didn't take it.

In 1970 ninety-nine of the one hundred job. Her loss of income after having a baby might mean she would not be able to pay back her loan. As a result, said historian Sara Evans, the credit industry "consistently marked women as "poor risks." If a husband or father cosigned the application, then he was promising to pay back the loan if the woman could not. That sort of reasoning, however, didn't quite fit with employment statistics. In 1970

Sandra Day O'Connor . . . graduated at the top of her class from law school too. A Los Angeles law firm offered her a job— as a legal secretary. She didn't take it.

U.S. senators were male. Only ten women served in the House of Representatives. And in the almost two-hundred-year history of the U.S. government, no woman had ever served on the Supreme Court.

Lower wages and limited education and employment opportunities for women were among the issues NOW hoped to bring to the nation's attention. In 1970 a woman usually could not apply for a bank loan to buy a car or a house unless she had the signature of a husband or father. Most consumer credit companies considered women to be poor risks. Why? Credit is given on a promise that the person will pay back the loan, with interest. A woman might marry, have a baby, and then leave her approximately one-half of all women were working outside the home. And more women remained in the workplace after marriage and pregnancy than in previous decades. Society once believed that women worked to earn cash for little luxury items—what some people called pin money. Increasingly in the 1970s and through the end of the century, however, many women worked for the same reasons men worked—to pay for food, clothing, and housing. There was a difference between working men and women, however. *Time* magazine reported that more working women than men lived in poverty.

Feminists argued that the media's portrayal of women differed from its portrayal of men. Advertisers, in particular, often used images and words that were demeaning to women, they said. Silva Thins's 1967 television commercial was one example. "Cigarettes are like girls," said the announcer. "The best ones are slim and rich." Even if it were true that the best men were slim and rich, no cigarette advertisement would ever have made that claim.

On the fiftieth anniversary of the Nineteenth Amendment, women still lacked many of the same rights as men. Betty Friedan was the president of NOW. What was needed was a national demonstration, she said, something so big it would make national headlines. NOW had only about five thousand members across the country. Even so, the members got to work spreading the word. They named their proposed national demonstration the Women's Strike for Equality. But would U.S. women, especially those who were not members of NOW, answer the call?

On August 26, 1970, in New York City, thousands of women participated in the strike. NOW had asked the city's mayor John Lindsay to close Fifth Avenue so the women could march. He refused. That day, as the women began moving forward, police on horseback tried to keep them on the sidewalks. But there were too many of them. They spilled onto the avenue, unfurling a banner that crossed three full lanes: "Women of the world unite." Betty Friedan linked arms with eighty-two-year-old Judge Dorothy Kenyon, and the march began. Dorothy Kenyon had been a young woman when suffragists won the right to vote. NOW had offered her a car to ride in during the parade. She preferred to walk. At one point, Friedan jumped up and down to see the end of the parade. She couldn't. Later estimates would confirm that as many as twenty thousand women had joined the march in New York City.

Judge Dorothy Kenyon, shown here testifying before the Senate Foreign Relations Subcommittee in 1950, remained active all her life in the fight for human rights, women's rights, and civil rights.

Some women carried posters. Some women carried their babies. "Don't iron while the strike is hot" read one poster. "I am not a Barbie doll" read another, protesting the images in women's fashion magazines. "Storks fly, why can't stewardesses?" read still another, questioning the policy of major airlines to force airline stewardesses who became pregnant to quit their jobs.

In Rochester, New York, women did more than toss aside their dish towels. They broke their dishes in a public demonstration. In Berkeley, California, women did not leave the dirty pots and pans in the sink but instead tied them on their backs as they marched down the street. In Boston, Massachusetts, a secretary wore a large cardboard typewriter over her clothes. In a New Jersey shopping mall parking lot, a mom wearing a sleeveless sundress and high heels wheeled her baby daughter in a stroller. On the stroller handle was a hand-printed sign that read, "Will I ever have the chance to be president?"

Women held banners high in Detroit, Michigan, and Saint Louis, Missouri:

"We have the right to vote (for the man of our choice)."

"We are the 51% minority."

"Housewives are slave laborers."

Men marched too. A few supported the women. Many more did not. Some of the men held signs of their own:

> *"We are the 51% minority."*
>
> —Protest sign based on the title of a 1970 essay by Robin Morgan

"We love women in the kitchen. . . ."

"End token equality."

"Draft women."

In fact, many Americans feared that if the "women's libbers" (as the media had begun to call supporters of the women's liberation movement) got their way, then the military would draft women into military service and send them into combat. The government was drafting only men to fight in the Vietnam War (1957–1975).

Not all of the approximately twenty thousand women who showed up on August 26, 1970, for the New York City rally of the National Organization for Women were supporters of its president, Betty Friedan (left). A contingent known as the Lavender Menace (right) demonstrated against the NOW leader's deliberate distancing from lesbian feminists, a stance that was reversed the following year.

Not all women who came to the demonstration marched. Many stood on the sidelines as spectators. Some women were puzzled by the whole liberation movement. "I don't know what those women are thinking of," said a female real estate agent in Los Angeles. "I love the idea of looking delectable and having men whistle at me."

One woman in Santa Barbara, California, proposed a counterdemonstration. She called it a National Celebration of Womanhood Day. Instead of marching in the streets with pots, pans, and typewriters, however, she suggested that each woman "wear her most frilly, feminine dress and . . . sing before breakfast." She should also serve her husband breakfast in bed.

The women's strike was a major news story, just as the women of NOW had hoped. Newspapers, magazines, and television networks reported on the day's events. The story the media told, however, was not particularly positive.

That evening CBS television news commentator Eric Sevareid quoted a recent poll that found two-thirds of American women did not believe they were oppressed. He compared the women's movement to an infectious disease. On ABC, news anchor Howard K. Smith ended his report on the march by quoting Senator Jennings Randolph of West Virginia. The senator, said

Smith, thought the women's movement was nothing more than "a band of braless bubbleheads."

Midge Kovacs was one of the women who marched that day. At night she turned on her television set to watch the news coverage of the event. She tuned in one channel and then another. She could hardly believe what she was hearing and seeing. The images were biased, sensationalized. The reporters focused on women who were so angry that they seemed to hate men, such as a woman whose poster read, "Don't cook dinner. Starve a rat tonight." Kovacs said, "Cameras moved in for tight shots of stringy haired, braless women in T-shirts, with angry signs. With my own eyes, I had seen a cross section of women at the march, including establishment types, career women and many older citizens, but none of these women were represented that evening on TV."

The 1910 suffragist (above) and the women at the 1970 rally (facing page) may look very different from each other. But they share a common goal: the desire for equality under the law.

the Women's Strike for Equality was the largest demonstration by women in the country's history. It started a second wave of feminism. The first wave was the one in which Judge Dorothy Kenyon had participated—the efforts of suffragists in the nineteenth and early twentieth centuries to win voting rights for women. Those who marched on August 26, 1970, did so to achieve additional rights: to earn the same wages as men, keep their maiden names when they married, practice birth control, and much more. Meanwhile, another group of feminists had been working toward women's equality in another way—by writing new laws and lobbying members of Congress to pass those laws. These were generally older women. Some were attorneys. Some held public office or worked in government organizations. Together, these two groups would change the way American society viewed women and even how women viewed themselves.

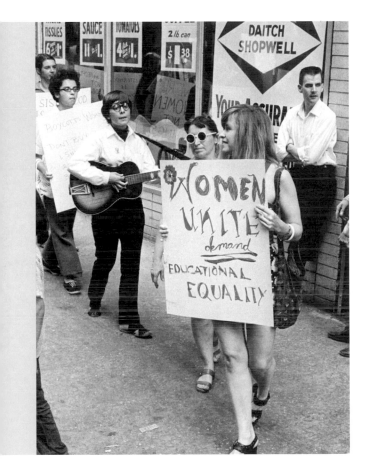

"Women's liberation is the liveliest conversational topic around," wrote a journalist in *Life* magazine. The magazine predicted that no matter what one's position was on equal rights, a women's movement was under way and gaining momentum. *Life* called it a "revolution that will affect every-body." This second wave of the women's movement would indeed rumble like thunder across society. From the 1970s through the end of the century, women's rights and their role in society would figure in often heated debates. The issues ranged widely, including poverty, homelessness, health and fitness, violence, and sexual harassment.

But feminism wasn't the only *ism* that influenced women's lives in the last three decades of the twentieth century. Materialism, too, shook up society's expectations for and about women. One of the hottest pop stars of the 1980s was Madonna, whose hit song "Material Girl" resonated with young women across the country. Girls wanted more than love and family. They wanted more than equal opportunity in the workplace too. They wanted money and all the goodies money could buy. For many women, being a material girl was more rewarding than being a feminist.

M̲s. and the Material Girls is the fifth and final volume in a series of books on the images and issues that influenced American women during the twentieth century. It is a journey back through the last three decades of the century to examine how popular culture portrayed women—the feminists, the antifeminists, and the material girls.

Chapter One

Who Took the **R** out of "M**R**s."?

It seems absurd to ask a woman, "How does it feel to be married to a working husband?" The assumption is that all men work outside the home. But ask a man, "How does it feel to have a working wife?" and you have a subject for university seminars, TV talk shows and a year's worth of dinner-party conversations. Someday this question will seem absurd also. But for now . . . .

— *"The Working Woman,"* Ladies' Home Journal, *March 1975*

Gloria Steinem, 1965

"A new hat—rather a bonnet—

was tossed into the presidential race today," reported Walter Cronkite on the CBS evening news in 1972. Approximately ten "hats" had been tossed into the presidential race already, all owned by white men. The bonnet metaphor, however, was Cronkite's way of saying that this wasn't just another male politician running for office. This hat belonged to a woman: Shirley Chisholm. She was also African American.

Chisholm was a controversial individual. When she first ran for the U.S. Congress in 1968, many people advised her to stick to teaching. Teaching was a woman's profession. Chisholm didn't listen, and she won the election. Once in Washington, D.C., she was an outspoken feminist who fought for justice for people of color and all American women. "We have to attack racism and sex-ism at the same time," she said. "These are two evils."

On January 25, 1972, Chisholm returned to her hometown of Brooklyn, New York. In the Concord Baptist Church, she told her constituents in a clear, confident voice, "I stand before you today as a candidate for the Democratic nomination for the presidency of the United States. I am not the candidate of black America, although I am black and proud. I am not the candidate of the women's movement of this country, although I am equally proud of that. I am not the candidate of any political bosses or special interests. I am the candidate of the people."

In reporting on her announcement, *Time* magazine didn't mention any bonnets, but it didn't give her much of a chance of winning. "Whatever happens, her bravado is

On January 5, 1972, U.S. representative Shirley Chisholm of Brooklyn, New York, announced her entry into the race for the Democratic nomination for U.S. president. The first African American woman elected to Congress, Chisholm, during her first term, hired an all-female staff and spoke out for civil rights, women's rights, and the poor—and against the Vietnam War.

impressive," *Time* stated. The odds of her winning the Democratic nomination for president were, in her own words, hopeless. But the campaign wasn't about her, she insisted. It was about raising awareness of women's issues and issues of race. Winning wasn't as important, she said, as running.

In March, *Time* speculated on the kind of woman who might become president and what implications a woman president could have for the country. Unfortunately, the stereotypes about women were still evident. "Should she be married? Would it make any difference?" asked the reporter. What if, the article continued, she were "sexy"? Would that alienate other women who would be jealous of her beauty? What if she had a baby? How would motherhood affect her ability to lead the country? Would she ignore military issues and focus instead on more nurturing programs, such as health care, child care, and education reform? *Time* predicted that no matter what kind of woman got elected, jokes would abound about who wore the pants in the White House.

Shirley Chisholm's candidacy broke new ground not only for women but also for African Americans. Here she is shown with fellow Democratic presidential nomination candidates appearing on Meet the Press *in July 1972. In the top row from left to right are Senators George McGovern, Hubert Humphrey, and Edmund Muskie. Sitting next to Chisholm is Senator Henry Jackson.*

The Democratic Party more or less ignored Chisholm's candidacy. At one point, the congresswoman filed a complaint with the Federal Communications Commission in order to participate in a televised debate featuring two of the Democratic front-runners: George McGovern and Hubert Humphrey.

> "I ran for the Presidency to demonstrate the sheer will and refusal to accept the status quo."
>
> —Shirley Chisolm, 1973

"I ran for the Presidency to demonstrate the sheer will and refusal to accept the status quo," Chisholm wrote in her 1973 book *The Good Fight*. "The next time a woman runs, or a black, or a Jew or anyone from a group that the country is 'not ready' to elect to its highest office, I believe that he or she will be taken seriously from the start. . . . I ran because somebody had to do it first."

Although George McGovern won the Democratic nomination that summer, Shirley Chisholm also won a victory. She had raised the country's consciousness about race and gender issues. The mayor of New York City went on record to praise the congresswoman's campaign. "She gave voice to the aspirations of millions in a system that excludes women and minority groups from full expression and equal opportunity, not only in politics but also in the economic and social life of the nation," he stated.

Change would take time, but Chisholm had planted the seeds of change. In time, those seeds would grow. Meanwhile, she was heading back to Congress to continue shaking up the system.

Jane Crow Laws

Other women were also shaking up the system. Pauli Murray and Martha Griffiths were among those older activists who had fought in the 1940s through the 1960s for civil rights as well as for women's rights.

In the 1940s, Pauli Murray was one of only a few female law students at Howard University, an African American university in Washington, D.C. The first day of class, her professor laughingly told the male students that he had no idea why women were admitted to the study of law. Since they were, he had no choice but to put up with them. Pauli Murray never forgot the laughter that followed. "I was too humiliated to respond," she said. "Later I began to notice that no matter how well prepared I was or how often I raised my hand, I seldom got to recite."

Were the professors deliberately ignoring her? She didn't think so. "The men's deeper voices," she said, "seemed to obliterate my lighter voice. . . . For much of that first year I was condemned to silence unless the male students exhausted their arguments or were completely stumped by a professor's question."

What Is Sexist Language?

One of Shirley Chisholm's campaign buttons reads "Ms. Chis. for Pres." Unlike *Mrs.* or *Miss*, *Ms.* does not reveal a woman's marital status. For that reason, many feminists adopted the title. After all, the feminists argued, *Mr.* doesn't reveal a man's marital status.

The feminist movement of the 1970s challenged other uses of language, as well. Why use the word *mankind* when *society* worked just as well, they argued. *Mankind* suggested women were invisible. *Fireman*, *policeman*, and *chairman*—such words likewise emphasized male dominance, they said. *Firefighter*, *police officer*, and *chairperson* did not.

In the 1970s, language and gender sparked debate and often ridicule. At the same time that women argued that *fireman* and *policeman* suggested that only men could fight fires or protect people, *Time* magazine joked that perhaps a *manhole* cover in a street should be renamed a *person hole* cover so as not to offend women. *Time* also suggested changing the spelling of *women* to *womyn*. That never officially happened, but lots of language changes did—textbooks were revised to remove sexist (and racist) language. Job announcements were reworded to include female as well as male applicants.

Sexist language also includes demeaning or insulting words or phrases. If terms such as *man-made* (why not *machine-made* instead?) annoyed feminists, they got downright angry when called a *babe*, a *broad*, or a *chick*. Babe

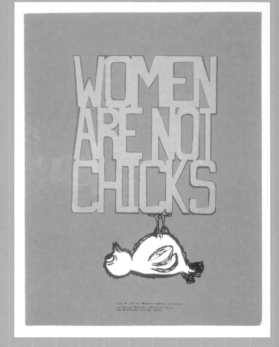

The 1971 "Women are not chicks" poster above reflects women's growing impatience with sexist language. By 1975 feminists confronted the use of thet word *girl* with posters such as the one below. The campaign worked. Shopgirls and office girls and even Girl Fridays eventually began to be referred to as working women.

suggested the woman was a child or a plaything, and the others suggested domestic animals. (Originally, *broad* meant a pregnant cow.) Under the same umbrella were labels such as *fox, lamb, kitten*, and *honey bunny*. Old women who talked a lot were *hens*. Women journalists were *news hens*. Many in society believed that a *henpecked* man was a weak man who couldn't confront and control his wife.

Of course, angry feminists did some name-calling of their own too. They called men who treated women as inferiors or who used sexist language on purpose *male chauvinist pigs*. (Chauvinists believe their group is superior to others.)

Sexist language appeared in television commercials too. National Airlines spent more than nine million dollars in the early 1970s on an advertising campaign called "Fly Me." A beautiful woman in a stewardess uniform told the television audience her name: "I'm Margie. Fly Me." Other beautiful women with other names made the same invitation. The company gave "Fly Me" pins to their stewardesses to wear on their uniforms. Some refused, charging the airline with sexism. Why couldn't the slogan be "Fly with us?" asked stewardess Ilene Held. That suggested flying with the airline rather than a sexual invitation from a stewardess. Although NOW took National Airlines to court, a judge upheld the airlines' right to run the Fly Me commercials.

Photographs of beautiful stewardesses (as they were known in 1970) and sexually suggestive language proved such an embarrassment to National Airline's employees that they sued (unsuccessfully) their employer to stop the very successful ad campaign.

Law school was not the first time Pauli Murray had confronted prejudice in a classroom. Years earlier, as the lone African American student in a class at New York's all-female Hunter College, she seethed at the way her professor ignored African American contributions to history. At Hunter College, she experienced racism. At Howard University, she experienced sexism. She became determined to use her law degree to fight both.

In the 1940s and 1950s, Murray did just that. She worked to erase Jim Crow laws off state and county law books. These were laws dating to the 1800s that segregated blacks from whites in public areas. In some towns, for example, restrooms and water fountains had signs that indicated "whites only" and "colored." Waiting rooms of train stations, seating in movie theaters, and even cemeteries were segregated by race. The same year Murray entered law school, she was forced to enter a "blacks only" entrance to a funeral home.

In the 1960s, Murray identified what she called Jane Crow laws. In some states, women could not serve on juries. In others they could not work in an establishment that served alcohol. Laws limited the number of hours a woman could work, usually not longer than an eight-hour day. Such limitations meant that women who needed extra income could not legally work overtime. In Pennsylvania a state law required the maximum penalty for a woman

Feminist, poet, professor, civil rights advocate, and attorney, the Reverend Dr. Pauli Murray was ordained as the first African American female Episcopal priest in 1977.

convicted of a felony. But it did not mandate maximum penalties for convicted male felons.

In 1970 Murray addressed a committee of the U.S. House of Representatives and presented her observations about discrimination against women. "Discrimination because of one's sex is just as degrading, dehumanizing, immoral, unjust, indefensible, infuriating, and capable of producing societal turmoil as discrimination because of one's race," she said. "One spends 50 years of one's life trying to get equal civil rights because of one's race and turns around and finds one must spend the second 50 years, if you should live so long, to get one's rights because of sex," she said.

Like Pauli Murray, Martha Wright Griffiths held a law degree. She was the first woman to serve as a judge in Detroit, Michigan. She later won election to the U.S. House of Representatives. In Congress she argued that women should receive the same benefits as men from Social Security. She supported free school lunch programs for children of the poor. *Time* magazine called Griffiths "the most persistent feminist in the U.S. Congress."

The U.S. Supreme Court ensures "equal justice under the law." Those words are chiseled in marble above the Supreme Court building. But justice wasn't always equal for women, Griffiths argued. The Supreme Court in 1938 had "forced the admission of a Negro to the University of

Elected to Congress in 1954, Representative Martha Griffiths was the first woman member of the House Ways and Means Committee. She used her influence to have women included in the Civil Rights Act of 1964, a key piece of legislation that addressed equal rights in areas such as voting, employment, and access to public education and federally assisted programs.

Missouri Law School," she told *Time*. Twenty years later, she pointed out, the Court did not intervene when Texas A&M University rejected the applications of two Texas women who hoped to study science.

Women such as Shirley Chisholm, Pauli Murray, and Martha Griffiths believed that significant changes could be made for women's equality by working through the legal system. Their approach was not to hold public demonstrations—though many took part in them. Rather, they lobbied politicians, meeting with them to explain their positions and viewpoints. They wrote legislation. They argued legal cases.

As these women pressed forward, popular culture began to reflect the changing times. Women's magazines such as *Vogue* and *Ladies' Home Journal* (*LHJ*) published stories on women's issues, including careers, education, and child care. *Glamour* ran features on self-assertiveness, including "How to Get More from Your Job" and "How to Start Doing What You Are Too Scared to Do." The editors of *Redbook* stated in a series on the feminist movement, "We believe that every human being should have the right and opportunity to make her or his own choices in every area of life."

Women communicated their viewpoints in other ways—through art, music, and writing. In the early 1970s, more than five hundred feminist newsletters, books, and magazines began rolling off presses with titles such as *Up from Under, Off Our Backs, Earth's Daughters,* and *Sisterhood is Powerful.* The viewpoints varied from one publication to another—testimony that the women's movement reached diverse groups of women.

Sisterhood is Powerful
AN ANTHOLOGY OF WRITINGS FROM THE WOMEN'S LIBERATION MOVEMENT

Edited by Robin Morgan

Former child actor and poet Robin Morgan wrote Sisterhood is Powerful *(1970), one of the first anthologies of feminist writings. In later years, she followed up on the theme with* Sisterhood is Global *(1984) and* Sisterhood is Forever *(2003).*

The Ms. Experiment

At first glance, *Ms.* looked like any other women's magazine on the newsstands. *Ms.*, however, was a magazine with an attitude significantly different from *Ladies' Home Journal*, *McCall's*, and *Cosmopolitan*. Like those popular women's magazine, *Ms.* had colorful photographs, glossy pages, advertisements, and "how-to" articles. But the cover girl wasn't a model—the July 1973 issue featured comic-strip heroine Wonder Woman. And the how-to articles were not about baking cakes or casseroles or winning the heart of a man. They were more likely to be about how to work with a car's internal combustion engine or how to win a much-deserved promotion in the office. One column titled "How to Make Trouble" told readers how to start a consciousness-raising group. The goal of consciousness-raising was to increase awareness of personal and social issues through small-group discussions, readings, or public protests.

Ms. was different in another way. In the 1970s, publishing was a male-dominated industry. Most popular magazines—whether published for men or women—were managed by men. *Ms.*, on the other hand, was managed by women. Writer Gloria Steinem was one of the founders of *Ms.* and eventually became the magazine's editor. Steinem

The first issue of Ms. *magazine made a statement, not only with its bold cartoon art of Wonder Woman running for president but also with its editorial content. Articles on topics such as the housewife's moment of truth, "de-sexing" the English language, and abortion caused news anchor Harry Reasoner to comment, "I'll give it six months before they run out of things to say." He was wrong.*

described Ms. as a "how-to magazine for the liberated female human being—not how to make jelly but how to seize control of your life."

In January 1972, 300,000 copies of the magazine's preview issue arrived at newsstands across the country. Within eight days, every copy had sold and approximately

From the early 1970s onward, Ms. *offered its readers editorial content that was quite different from other women's magazines, such as* Vogue *(right),* which focused solely on fashion, beauty, or homemaking. Articles in the 1973 issue of Ms. (left) include job advice, the morning-after pill, and the ecological outlook of the telephone company. While the fashion magazines' covers always featured beautiful women, Ms. covers tended toward more thought-provoking graphics.

thirty-six thousand readers had subscribed for future issues. A successful magazine needs more than readers, however. The money that floats commercial magazines comes not from the money readers pay to purchase a copy but rather from advertisements. Advertising was still another way *Ms.* differed from other magazines. The publishers accepted only ads that realistically portrayed women. Women did not, for example, spend half their income on perfumes, shampoos, and lipsticks, wrote the editors in the July 1972 issue. Nor did

they spend half on hamburgers. Women bought stereos, televisions, automobiles, and even tools—those were the sorts of products *Ms.* wanted as advertisements. The editors promised too to reject any advertisement with words or images that suggested women were like children who needed a man's protection or like goddesses who tempted men into romantic affairs.

Virginia Slims cigarettes was very interested in running its full-page ads "You've come a long way, baby" in *Ms.* The female staff objected. Women weren't babies. They suggested a new slogan: "You'll go a long way." The company refused. And so, true to their word, *Ms.* editors turned down the Virginia Slims account, even though it would have earned the struggling magazine a great deal of much-needed income.

By December 1972, *Ms.* had increased its subscriptions to an impressive 160,000 and was selling an additional 235,000 issues at newsstands. The magazine was making a profit. It was, reported *Time* magazine, "a situation almost unheard of in modern publishing." The media seemed as much impressed with editor Gloria Steinem as it did with the new magazine. She appeared on the cover of *McCall's. Newsweek* devoted a full paragraph to describing her physical appearance, citing her long, blonde-streaked hair and miniskirts. She was a "feminist who looked like a fashion model." The media made a point to emphasize that Steinem was single "by choice." Suddenly a single career woman seemed like a very good thing to be, especially if the woman looked like Gloria Steinem.

Gloria Steinem's good looks were what initially drew media attention to her. But it was her keen intellect and quick wit that made her a feminist spokesperson. She is responsible for such quips as "A woman without a man is like a fish without a bicycle," "Some of us are becoming the men we want to marry," or, when commenting on marriage, "I don't breed well in captivity."

Gee, Charlie and Smitty Smell Terrific!

Advertisers jumped on the women's liberation bandwagon in the 1970s. Even products that seemingly had nothing to do with women's rights, such as deodorants, suddenly took on a feminist tone.

"How Do You Rate as a 1973 Woman?" was the headline of a full-page antiperspirant ad in a 1973 issue of *Mademoiselle*. The text continued: "It used to be a man's world. But you've changed it. . . .

Helen Reddy Roars

Helen Reddy disliked what she called the doormat songs. They were popular songs about women who love their men even though the men cheat on them, stay out late and, in general, walk all over them. For instance, in the 1960s, Joanie Sommers sang "Johnny Get Angry." The lyrics told Johnny that a girl wanted a guy who was possessive and jealous because that proved he loved her. In another song, Sandy Posey sang, "If you're born a woman, you're born to be hurt." The boy in this song treats his girlfriend "mean." But when he shows up— and she often doesn't know when that will be—she welcomes him home because she loves him.

Those kinds of songs weren't what Reddy wanted to sing. In 1970 the singer-songwriter from Australia was living in California and going to feminist meetings. She wrote a song titled "I Am Woman." The lyrics were controversial because the song wasn't about romance. It wasn't about men at all. It was, Reddy told a *Newsweek* interviewer, a "chest-beating" song of pride in being a woman. The song's chorus states: "If I have to, I can do anything. I am strong. I am invincible. I am woman."

Helen Reddy, shown here in 1975, was the cowriter and singer of "I Am Woman." She says she wrote the piece because she wanted to share the positive self-image she had gained from being part of the women's liberation movement. Recorded in 1971, the song eventually became the movement's unofficial anthem.

Helen Reddy recorded the song in May 1972, but radio stations across the country did not play it. Perhaps the station managers thought a song about female pride rather than romantic heartbreak wouldn't interest the American public. Or maybe the male-dominated radio industry simply thought it silly. Whatever the reason, without airtime, a song generally doesn't sell. "I Am Woman" was the exception. Reddy performed the song on television variety shows. The song was featured in a film, *Stand Up and Be Counted*. Suddenly, women across the country were calling radio stations asking to hear it. "I Am Woman" began selling as many as twenty-five thousand copies a day. By December 1972, the song hit number one on the *Billboard* magazine charts, making Reddy a star. The song became an anthem, a sort of pledge of allegiance, for feminists.

In a 1970s deodorant ad (above), *the man in the picture is the one who is sweating. In the 1980s* (above right), *an appreciative man is in the background, but the arrow is pointing to the woman's armpit to show that the perspiration is hers. By the 1990s* (right), *it was assumed that women sweated—after all, they played major competitive sports. Deodorant no longer had anything to do with pleasing a man.*

But now that you're tough enough to dish it out, you should be tough enough to take it. Frankly, you sweat. That's why you need an antiperspirant that's tough. . . . Hour after Hour. It fights odor and all three kinds of wetness. From heat, tension, and exercise. . . . Yet it has a new fragrance that tells you you're still utterly feminine."

In the 1960s, television advertisements for Secret deodorant had often portrayed women in traditional roles—a woman in a supermarket or a bride on the morning of her wedding. The advertisements had promised women that "icy blue" Secret would keep them cool and calm during moments of stress. In the 1970s, however, Secret altered its message to emphasize a woman's independence. In one TV commercial, a husband complains because his wife is packing too many unnecessary things for a weekend getaway. He picks up her deodorant and his own and asks why they need to pack both. "Why can't you use mine?" he asks. Shocked, she snatches her bottle of Secret away from him. "I can't go anywhere without my Secret," she tells him. OK, he agrees, he'll use her deodorant then. At this point, many a real woman might have told him to get over it! An extra bottle of deodorant doesn't take up much extra space. But in the world of television advertising, she smiles sweetly and delivers Secret's new slogan: "Secret is strong enough for a man, but made for a woman." And then she adds, "It smells pretty, too."

In the 1970s, the Revlon cosmetics company spent months interviewing women on what they liked best—and least—in a perfume. The company discovered that many liberated women disliked being told that a perfume could make them more attractive to men. From this research came Revlon's new fragrance, which they labeled Charlie. Although a male name, Revlon's Charlie was a liberated female who wore pantsuits to work rather than dresses. Model Shelley Hack portrayed Charlie in magazine ads. The images often showed her dashing across the street with a confident smile. Where Charlie was going didn't matter. That she was on the go did.

Charlie had a man's name and wore men's clothes—but that did not mean that she wasn't totally feminine. It just meant that Charlie was so together that she could do anything she pleased.

The advertising slogan, "She's so Charlie," was also intentionally vague. Was Charlie a person? Or was Charlie a description? Both, said Revlon. Charlie was an independent, fun-loving woman. She was also young and very pretty.

Perfume competitor Coty created a new fragrance of its own. The fragrance also had a masculine-sounding name, Smitty. The Smitty model looked amazingly like Charlie—blonde, slender, and white. In one magazine photograph, Smitty dances the night away while a handsome man nuzzles her neck. Smitty's advertising lingo was, "When you're feeling so free, everybody can see Smitty did it!" Coty described its fragrance as "spirited" and "sexy."

Whether a woman chose Hour After Hour or Secret, Charlie or Smitty, the message was much the same. Ads declared that liberated woman could also be feminine.

The Antifeminists Fire Back

Gloria Steinem believed equality for women would ultimately also benefit men. So she believed the press should call the women's liberation movement "humanism" (value for all humans) and not "feminism." But men—and many women—disagreed. Some, in fact, disagreed strongly. The same year that *Ms.* was selling every copy it printed, *Time* reported that men felt threatened by the new feminists. More young women were choosing not to marry. Many of those already married were no longer content with being housewives and mothers. Feminism "has transformed—and sometimes wrecked—marriages by ending once automatic assumptions about woman's place," the news magazine stated.

Antifeminists were those women and men who did not want U.S. Congress to pass the Equal Rights Amendment to the Constitution. They did not want government to interfere in family and home matters. Phyllis Schlafly was a famous antifeminist. She described feminists as antifamily and antichildren. *Ms.*, she said, was a "series of sharp-tongued, high-pitched, whining complaints by unmarried women."

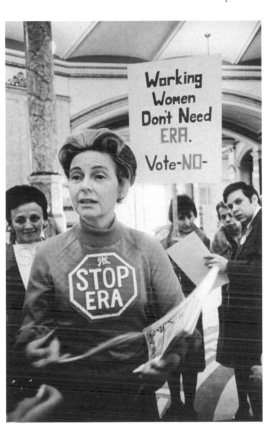

Phyllis Schlafly worked tirelessly to defeat the passage of the Equal Rights Amendment. Here she is shown in 1975 wearing a Stop ERA sign on her chest. She is leading a demonstration inside the Illinois state capitol while the state's legislature considers the amendment to the U.S. Constitution.

An ERA Timeline

The Nineteenth Amendment to the U.S. Constitution granted women the right to vote. Winning passage of that amendment had taken many decades. Many woman suffragists endured public ridicule for speaking out and marching for the right to vote. Others were arrested, and some were physically beaten. The hard-won victory came at last in 1920.

The right to vote, however, was not the same thing as having equal rights under the law. Another amendment was needed to eliminate discrimination based upon sex. In 1923 suffragist Alice Paul wrote and proposed the Lucretia Mott Amendment, named after one of the first American feminists. Often called the Equal Rights Amendment (ERA), it read: Equality of rights under the law shall not be denied or abridged by the United States or by any state on account of sex.

Just a single sentence, the proposed amendment was nevertheless controversial. Even though it was introduced in every session of Congress from 1923 to 1970, the amendment never came up for a vote. Men and women both argued against the ERA, fearing passage would threaten the fabric of society.

Alice Paul was one of the leading figures who worked toward the passage of the Nineteenth Amendment to the U.S. Constitution. Here she holds up a glass toward a suffrage banner to which stars had been added as individual states backed the cause.

In 1970 Martha Griffiths succeeded in bringing the ERA to the floor of Congress for a vote. In 1972 both the House of Representatives and the Senate passed the ERA. For an amendment to become federal law, however, thirty-eight of the fifty states must ratify (formally approve) it within a specific amount of time.

In 1977 Alice Paul died. By the end of that year, thirty-five states had ratified the amendment. The original author of the ERA must have believed that passage of the amendment was around the corner. But powerful opponents had begun fighting against it. Eventually, they would succeed. The ERA has never become law.

Schlafly captured the media's attention. "If Gloria Steinem and Betty Friedan want to call themselves *Ms.* in order to conceal their marital status, their wishes should be respected," Schlafly wrote in 1977. "But most married women feel they worked hard for the r in their names; and they don't care to be gratuitously deprived of it."

Schlafly was the mother of six children and a former librarian who had run unsuccessfully for Congress. She chose not to work because, she said, her family was her career. She didn't need to work to clothe and feed her family. Her husband was a successful lawyer who provided a good income for his family and, she said, "lets me do what I want to do." She also had a live-in housekeeper. Since 1967 Schlafly had been publishing a newsletter called the *Phyllis Schlafly Report*. In the 1970s, Schlafly turned her attention to the feminist movement with the specific goal of defeating the Equal Rights Amendment. The wording of the amendment, argued Schlafly, was a "smokescreen." Be warned, she wrote, "when feminists talk about 'women's rights,' they mean a radical restructuring of society, with government using its power to force feminist goals on all the rest of us." She took her "Stop ERA" campaign to the media. She appeared on television talk shows. She spoke to women's groups. And in her newsletters, she continued to describe the disastrous consequences should the ERA become a federal law.

What were those dire consequences antifeminists dreaded? One was military service. In the United States in the 1970s, women did not fight alongside men on the battlefield. If men and women were equal in *all* things, the antifeminists argued, then Congress would

> If men and women were equal in all things, the antifeminists argued, then Congress would draft women into military service and send them into combat.

draft women into military service and send them into combat. Other predictions were equally shocking to some in society. A woman who wished to terminate a pregnancy would be able to do so by constitutional right and without the permission of the child's father. Prisons would no longer be segregated by sex. Hospital rooms, schools, and public facilities such as restrooms would also become unisex. Even separate organizations for Boy Scouts and Girl Scouts would cease to exist.

These were the predicted consequences. No one knew for certain what the social changes might actually be. But Marion Olson, an antifeminist from Minnesota, was convinced the ERA would change the very concepts of womanhood and manhood. "We don't want to turn our daughters into tigers and our sons into pansies," she told *Time* magazine in 1973. In Olson's opinion, the ERA would do just that. "Nature did not intend men and women to be equal," Olson stated.

Antifeminists held rallies. They paraded in streets with banners and buttons that read "Stop ERA" and "ERA is a crushing blow to American families." They wrote to their congressmen—and the few congresswomen who held office. The antifeminist voices were loud and determined. One North Carolina woman expressed her objection to equal rights regardless of sex coming on top of equal rights regardless of race. She said, "*Forced* busing [of minority students to integrate schools], *forced* mixing, *forced* hiring. Now forced *women. No thank you.*"

A group of men demonstrate in 1970 on behalf of extending the draft to include women. (At the time, all U.S. adult men could be drafted into military service through a lottery system.)

Schlafly's efforts turned the tide against the Equal Rights Amendment. *Time* magazine called her "feminine but forceful." Even her foes—the feminists—admitted she was "an incredibly shrewd activist." Author Susan Douglas, who supported the ERA, went so far as to say Schlafly had "single-handedly" defeated the amendment.

The defeat came in 1982, when the amendment's time ran out. Although thirty-five of the necessary thirty-eight states had originally ratified the amendment, under pressure from Schlafly and the antifeminists, several states repealed their approval. Although the ERA had died, *Ms.* was still attempting to liberate women's lives each month. Steinem and other feminists were not going away. But neither were Schlafly and her supporters.

The Ferraro Factor

A decade after Shirley Chisholm ran for president of the United States, another congresswoman made national headlines and U.S. political history. In 1984 Democratic presidential nominee Walter Mondale asked Geraldine Ferraro to be his vice-presidential running mate. His choice was controversial. Never before had a major U.S. political party nominated a woman to the presidential ticket. But this time, a party had chosen a qualified woman because she was a woman. Ferraro admitted that had she been a man, Mondale would not have chosen her. *Time* magazine agreed. "Fate and gender, not her résumé, put Ferraro on the ticket."

Why did Mondale choose a woman? The media speculated on the answer. Mondale was running against a conservative Republican president, Ronald Reagan. Public polls showed Mondale to be the underdog, trailing behind the popular Reagan. Ferraro was a liberal-minded congresswoman from New York. Elected to the House of Representatives in 1978, she had supported the ill-fated Equal Rights Amendment. She was pro-choice—she believed a woman had a right to decide whether to terminate a pregnancy. If nothing else, Geraldine Ferraro would generate a great deal of media attention. And she did.

If nothing else, Geraldine Ferraro would generate a great deal of media attention. And she did.

Dressing for Success

"Fact: Most American men dress for failure." This was the opening line in John Molloy's best-selling nonfiction book *Dress for Success*. Published in 1975, the book focused on professional men. Selecting the right clothes and colors increased a man's chances of getting a job or being promoted to a better-paying position, the author claimed.

According to Molloy, letting your wife or girlfriends choose your clothing was "a suicidal mistake." What a woman finds attractive is not what an executive in a business office finds attractive. Molloy based this conclusion on a stereotype about women and the fashion industry. "The fact is that for years women have been indoctrinated by the fashion industry to believe that anything new, up-to-date, innovative and different is desirable," he wrote. In fact, Molloy claimed, men should dress conservatively.

Molloy divided a man's closet into two types of wardrobes, according to the hands on the clock. Before five in the afternoon, a man dresses for business success. After five he dresses for romantic success. In a chapter titled "How to Dress for Success with Women," Molloy once again used sweeping generalizations to explain what women between the ages of eighteen and thirty-five found attractive. "Most women like men with thin hips," he wrote. "Most women like men in open shirts."

What about working women? Molloy ignored them. (He'd get around to women's wardrobes a few years later.) Professional women, however, didn't ignore Molloy's book. Many adopted his advice. If the somber blue business suit was king, then the somber skirted blue business suit was queen. A man's most important status symbol was a tie, said Molloy. So women began wearing neckwear such as floppy bow ties too.

By 1979 *Glamour* magazine had published its own "dress for success" book for women. By then, reported the magazine's editors, 50 percent of all women worked outside the home. Through its research, *Glamour* discovered that interviewers of job applicants thought a woman who wore tailored pantsuits and her hair in a tight bun appeared "too inflexible" and was "denying her femininity." On the other hand, the woman in the baggy sweater and gaudy beads was just too trendy to be taken seriously. The best choice? A conservative dress or skirt.

By the 1980s, workplace fashions were changing. Sure, the somber blue suit with the floppy bow tie was conservative and safe, said fashion consultant Emily Cho. But women who wore those boring business uniforms looked like everyone else and risked fading into the wallpaper. "Molloy is wrong in *Dress for Success*," said Cho in her own 1983 book, *Looking, Working, Living Terrific 24 Hours a Day*. She recommended soft turtleneck dresses and rose-colored silk blouses. "Women have earned the right to relax into their femininity," she wrote.

Although styles and colors had changed for both men and women, one thing hadn't: people made judgments based on a person's appearance. Right or wrong, image remained important.

The early dress-for-success formula for women was to mirror the business dress of a man—a suit and shirt, and an ever-so-slightly feminized version of a necktie. Some designers for women made subtle changes to the male suit-and-tie costume as shown on this page. Others had great fun exaggerating the concept, coming up with outfits such as the one on the facing page.

New York congresswoman Geraldine Ferraro speaks at the July 1984 Democratic National Convention, where she was named Walter Mondale's vice-presidential running mate. She was the first woman to run for vice president on a major party ticket. In her acceptance speech, Ferraro said, "The daughter of an immigrant from Italy has been chosen to run for vice president in the new land my father came to love."

Ferraro was, reported *Time*, both feminine and feminist. Her short, blonde-frosted hair was stylish. She loved to shop, and she could flirt, the newsmagazine reported. She could also fight. "God help anyone who gets in her way," said Republican congresswoman Bobbi Fielder.

Walter Mondale and his campaign advisers had high expectations for their vice-presidential candidate. They wanted her to convince women—both feminists and antifeminists alike—to vote the Democratic ticket. Ferraro was also Catholic and of Italian ancestry. The campaign advisers hoped other Catholics and minority ethnic groups would vote for her as well. Those expectations were unrealistic, admitted John Sasso, the manager of the Mondale-Ferraro campaign. "Some people expected she would single-handedly sweep up all the ethnics, all the women," he said. "My god, that's three-quarters of the country."

During her acceptance speech at the 1984 Democratic National Convention, Ferraro commented on her historical nomination. "By choosing a woman to run for our nation's second highest office, you sent a powerful signal to all Americans. There are no doors we cannot unlock. We will place no limits on achievement."

The "Ferraro Factor" created a media sensation. But the Mondale-Ferraro ticket failed to convince the American people to change leadership in the White House. Ronald Reagan won reelection by a landslide.

A year later, an emotionally bruised Ferraro wrote in her autobiography that her three-month candidacy was thrilling but also deeply painful. She had been stunned and hurt by the "depth of the fury, the bigotry, and the sexism" triggered by her name on the ticket. Her religious beliefs, gender, finances, and personal life were attacked. "It was so endlessly annoying to be presumed as weak and indecisive simply because I was a woman," she said. Many years later, Ferraro would tell CNN (Cable News Network) that not letting women down was her greatest challenge. "If I failed, they would fail," she said. "It's a lot of pressure. It's pressure that they don't put on a man."

The Ferraro Factor had failed to win the election. But Geraldine Ferraro did not fail. Journalist Maureen Dowd believed Ferraro "handled her role as the first woman to run for the Vice Presidency with grit, intelligence and humor." *Time* magazine's political reporter William R. Doemer agreed. "She has almost certainly altered forever the role women will play in the U.S. political system."

"Some people expected she would single-handedly sweep up all the ethnics, all the women, My god, that's three-quarters of the country."

—John Sasso, 1984

CHAPTER TWO

Bionic Women
and REAL-LIFE HEROINES

I grew up in the 1970s. I watched *The Bionic Woman* and *Charlie's Angels* on television. My mother frowned at such programs and would ask me, with exasperation clear in her voice, "What do you see in them?". . . I was mesmerized because I saw them as different, particularly for women. *The Bionic Woman* got to rip a telephone book apart with her bare hands and run sixty miles (97 kilometers) an hour. The Angels solved mysteries and traveled to exotic places.

—Sherrie A. Inness in *Disco Divas* (2003)

In running for president,

Shirley Chisholm gave women and people of color a voice. In founding *Ms.*, Gloria Steinem used the pages of her magazine to communicate women's issues. Other voices spoke to women, as well, in the 1970s— female actors, athletes, and astronauts. Suddenly, the conflicts and challenges women faced became the subject of movie plots. *Turning Point* told the story of two young women, both ballerinas—one who pursues her career and the other who gives it up to raise a family. *An Unmarried Woman* explores a woman's attempt to piece her life together once her husband leaves her. In *Looking for Mr. Goodbar*, a single woman struggles to find love and self-esteem in a string of one-night romantic relationships. Said Gareth Wiggan, a vice president at Twentieth Century Fox movie studios, audiences of the 1970s wanted to see movies about relationships. "And if you want to do movies about relationships between people, you can't just have men. Women are people, too."

Television, too, had discovered that women—and not just married housewives—were an important audience. Mary Tyler Moore had played a housewife and mother in the popular 1960s TV sitcom *The Dick Van Dyke Show*. But in 1970, she starred in a new TV show reflecting changes in women's lives: *The Mary Tyler Moore Show*. Moore portrayed Mary Richards, a career woman. According to the show's theme song, she could "turn the world on with her smile." In this new TV comedy, Mary Richards moves to Minneapolis, Minnesota, and applies for a job as a secretary, but it is filled, so she is hired for a lower-paying job as an associate producer. Later, she is promoted to producer. She is a liberated woman, in part, because she has a career in what was then a typically male profession—broadcasting.

Mary Tyler Moore is shown in 1974 on the set of her highly successful sitcom, The Mary Tyler Moore Show. *The show ran for seven seasons and focused on the professional and personal life of a single working woman.* Charlie's Angels *(facing page), a TV show that ran from 1976 to 1981, focused on three sexy female detectives.*

She is also liberated because of her lifestyle. She chooses to remain single and lives alone in her own apartment. The weekly episodes focused on her working relationships in the newsroom and at home.

Mary Richards became a cultural icon of the 1970s. Women copied her hairstyle and clothing—fashionable but functional and not too expensive. No one in the fictional Minneapolis newsroom belittled Mary for not being a wife or mother. The program's theme song the first year asked, "How will you make it on your own?" Once the show became a big hit, the lyrics changed (in the second season) to "You're gonna make it after all." The audience understood that making it on your own meant without a husband. Images of Mary during the opening credits included a shot of her in a supermarket, seemingly frustrated over what to buy. But was she frustrated because she was

"You're gonna make it after all."
—*The Mary Tyler Moore Show* theme song

cooking for just herself and not a husband? Or did the scene mean she wasn't particularly thrilled to be cooking at all? Another image from the opening credits was less ambiguous. An enthusiastic and happy Mary Richards is walking along the city's streets when she impulsively tosses her winter cap into the air. It was a gesture of liberation.

Mary Richards was a nonthreatening feminist. Unlike Shirley Chisholm, she didn't call sexism a social evil. She didn't protest or walk off the job to strike for women's rights. Even so, her show made it OK for real working women to be single and make it on their own too. Being a single working woman became an accomplishment women could be proud of, reported the *New York Times* in 1974. Gone were the nasty labels of spinster and old maid. Single women of the 1970s were more "self-assured, confident, secure" than they had been ever been.

THE GYNOIDS

The women of Stepford are Barbie-doll beautiful. They coat their eyelashes with mascara and gloss their lips pink. Their hair is usually long and always perfectly curled and shiny. Instead of pantsuits and blue jeans, they wear flowery dresses and wide-brimmed hats, even if they are just wandering supermarket aisles. Joanna Eberhart, a new arrival in Stepford, is pretty, but she isn't perfect—nor does she want to be. When not pulled back in a rubber band, her long brown hair often hangs in

The women of the 1975 movie version of The Stepford Wives *dressed according to their husbands' instructions. They look more like a bridal party than a group of women doing their weekly shopping. The term* Stepford wife *has come to refer to a woman who is overly subservient to her husband's demands.*

her eyes. Her clothes are not perfectly ironed. Unlike her new neighbors, Joanna does not cook hot breakfasts for her family every morning and she doesn't get excited about scrubbing stains out of laundry.

Joanna is an aspiring photographer. Moving to Stepford wasn't her idea. Her husband insisted on leaving the bustling big city for a serene suburban community in New England. After the family settles in Stepford, however, he begins to change. He used to encourage his wife's photography career. He used to help Joanna to care for the children. He even shared the household chores. Instead, he criticizes her. And he spends a lot of time in Stepford's all-male community club.

Joanna soon discovers a disturbing conspiracy. The Stepford husbands are up to no good in their private club. They have figured out a way to turn their wives into gynoids, or humanlike female robots. (Male humanlike robots are called androids, although that term is sometimes applied to both genders.) Unless she escapes soon, Joanna too will become a plastic Barbie. "If I'm wrong, I'm insane," she says. "But if I'm not wrong . . ."

The movie *The Stepford Wives* was based on a science-fiction suspense novel published in 1972. Sci-fi stories often explore social issues, warning the world, beware! Unless society changes its ways, this could really happen! Did moviegoers leave the theater fearful that real husbands would one day replace their living, breathing wives with gynoids? Probably not. So what was the movie (and the book) warning against?

Released during the height of the women's liberation movement in 1975, the movie was supposed to appeal to feminists, reported the *New York Times*. Men (at least the arrogant ones in fictional Stepford) didn't like their women sloppy, outspoken, and independent. They liked them docile, adoring, and dependent. The film also might have been a warning to women. If you allow men to dominate you, then you already are a "Stepford wife."

"hey really do want wives who are robots."

—Gael Greene, *New York Times*, 1975

Columbia Studios held a special screening in New York City for one-hundred-women "opinion makers," eager for their endorsement. The opinion makers were feminists, including NOW president Betty Friedan and Elizabeth Harris, one of the founders of *Ms.* During the screening, however, the women hissed, groaned, and laughed, according to the newspaper. Betty Friedan walked out, but not before saying, "I don't think we should help publicize this movie. It's a rip-off of the women's movement."

"It dumps on everyone, women, men, suburbia," said writer Linda Arking, who also attended the screening. "I think it's completely ridiculous." Although most of the opinion makers that night agreed with Friedan and Arking, other women thought the film was thought provoking. Writer Gael Greene thought the Stepford husbands were like many men she knew. "They really do want wives who are robots."

The Bionic Beauty

Jaimie Sommers was a bionic woman rather than a gynoid. Her character appeared in the 1970s television program *The Six Million Dollar Man*. After a crash landing in the desert while testing a new aircraft, the show's main character, Steve Austin became a human guinea pig. Top-secret military doctors saved his life by replacing parts of his body—both legs, an arm, and an eye—with bionic, or mechanical, implants. In Secret Service circles, Steve became known as "the six million dollar man."

Lindsay Wagner played Austin's fiancée, a tennis professional named Jaimie Sommers. Tragedy strikes when her parachute fails to open while she's skydiving. Steve convinces government agents to save her life. Sommers, too, gets bionic body parts. As the bionic woman, Jaimie can outrun a speeding car and jump extremely high. Her

Actress Lindsay Wagner appears to hold a man in a Mini above her head during a June 1976 visit to London to promote her television series The Bionic Woman. *(This was before the days of computer photo alteration, and the car actually had to be held aloft by a cable, which was out of sight of the camera.)*

mechanical ear allows her to hear a whisper from far away. Unfortunately, Sommers becomes emotionally unstable due to a malfunction of her bionics. Too late, doctors discover her body is rejecting her mechanical implants.

And then . . . she dies. Or so the television audience believed. Sensing they might have a profitable spin-off (based in part on the amount of fan mail Jaimie received), the ABC television studios later rewrote the story. Jaimie survives to become the lead in her own TV show, *The Bionic Woman*.

Do the Six Million Dollar Man and the Bionic Woman rekindle their love? Not in the liberated seventies! In deciding to give the Bionic Woman her own television series, the show's producers took away more than her tennis racket. She loses her memory and all knowledge of being in love with Steve Austin.

ALLEY CATS AND ANGELS

Action-adventure series on television have always drawn big audiences—at least for TV producer Aaron Spelling, who created police shows such as *The Rookie* and *Starsky and Hutch* in the 1970s. The stories focused on crime in the gritty big city. While brainstorming ideas for still another hit TV series, Spelling wondered what might happen if the cops weren't male but female. The producer wasn't interested so much in everyday policewomen in blue uniforms with caps. Instead, he conjured up a trio of young and very beautiful undercover detectives.

The premise for the weekly shows was that three policewomen who were very capable at crime detection got only boring and safe police assignments, such as writing traffic tickets and typing reports. A mysterious man named Charlie (unseen—only his voice is heard) hires the three women to work for him as private detectives. The policewomen—Sabrina the smart one, Kelly the sweet one, and Jill the sexy one—are all beautiful and single. When Charlie calls, they slip into comfortable and fashionable clothes and, more important, they confront mean criminals and solve crimes rather than read parking meters.

Stars (left to right) *Jaclyn Smith, Kate Jackson, and Farrah Fawcett pose for a promotional shot for their successful yet controversial television series* Charlie's Angels. *While feminists appreciated the women's competence, they criticized a male boss calling the shots as well as the character's sexy demeanors.*

Aaron Spelling called the new program *The Alley Cats*. Alley cats are streetwise strays, tough felines who know how to survive in the city. Perhaps Spelling envisioned his women detectives to be just as scrappy and independent. When the program premiered in the fall of 1976, however, it had a different name, *Charlie's Angels*. The word *angel* conjures a much different image than the term *alley cat*. An angel is pure, pious, and protective. Despite the name change (or perhaps because of it), the show was an overnight sensation. Millions of viewers tuned in each Wednesday evening.

Unlike previous shows that featured females as the lead characters, *Charlie's Angels* was equally popular with men and women. ABC figured women would tune in to see what the angels were wearing while men would tune in to see what they *weren't* wearing. *Time* magazine reported that a typical *Angels* script had at least one of the detectives appearing on-screen in a bathing suit (often a bikini) within the first ten minutes. More often than not, however, the angels dressed for success as real-life liberated women were doing—in long-sleeved blouses, blazers, and pants.

endless promises to clean my room in return for the rare privilege of staying up to watch the show." Even though her parents usually said no, *Charlie's Angels* became a big influence in her life. After school she and her friends pretended to be the angels, solving neighborhood crimes. "I always chose to play Sabrina—the smartest and coolest of the angels. I eventually cajoled my family into buying me Charlie's Angels paper dolls, action figures, and trading cards . . . lunch-box and Halloween costume (a Sabrina mask, of course.)"

Womack might have owned many of the toys associated with the program, but as a child, she was unaware of the social controversy that swirled about the angels. Some men and women applauded ABC's decision to create an action-adventure show starring women and to give them careers in a

> ***T**ime* **magazine reported that a typical Angels script had at least one of the detectives appearing on-screen in a bathing suit (often a bikini) within the first ten minutes.**

Whitney Womack was just six years old in 1976, the year *Charlie's Angels* premiered on television. Her parents made her go to bed before the show came on. "I remember begging and pleading," she said, "making

male-dominated profession—police work. The characters were intelligent and strong. However, many feminists bristled with indignation. Why must the women work for and take orders from a man? And why did every program focus so much on the trio's "jiggling" bodies? Journalist Judith Coburn believed *Charlie's Angels* only pretended to be about liberated women. Instead, she said, it kept alive "the myth that women always use sex to get what they want, even on the job." An angry reader of *Time* magazine agreed with Judith Coburn. "*Charlie's Angels*," she wrote the editors, was "a giant step backward for womanhood."

But that's not how Sarah Vowell viewed Sabrina, Kelly, and Jill. As a child, she watched *Charlie's Angels*. Years later, she would become a journalist and a best-selling author. She admitted that the first fan letter she ever wrote was to Farrah Fawcett, the actress who played Angel Jill. To Vowell, Jill and her two crime-fighting friends were as much alley cats as they were angels. "With apologies to Gloria Steinem," Vowell wrote many years later, referring to the Ms. magazine founder, "I think *Charlie's Angels* along with *The Bionic Woman* and *Wonder Woman* made me a feminist."

WOMEN MAKE NEWS, 1973—BILLIE JEAN KING'S GRAND SLAM

He dared her to do it. He told the national media that she couldn't do it because she was a woman and he was a man. She was Billie Jean King, a tennis champion. He was Bobby Riggs, and he had also been a champion tennis player when he was younger. He was the king of hustle, meaning he loved media attention and he knew just how to get it. The women's liberation movement was a tool he used to seek the celebrity spotlight.

Lynda Carter played Wonder Woman *(above) from 1976 through 1979 in the television series of the same name. The character was created in December 1941 by William Moulton Marston, a Harvard-educated psychologist. Marston launched the comic-book character as a woman who would fight fascism and also challenge the male-dominated world of superheroes.*

Real, Not Reel, Policewomen

Captain George Emil didn't much like hiring women. He wasn't the only one in the San Francisco Police Department who felt that way in 1975. Emil said, "99 and 44/100 percent of police officers don't believe women have the physical ability to deal with violent situations. But we're going to do exactly what the judge tells us." The judge was enforcing Title VII of the Civil Rights Act of 1964, which prohibits discrimination in hiring based on race, gender, sex, and national origin.

Female police officers were not a new phenomenon: Los Angeles, California, had hired its first policewoman in 1910. However, prior to 1972, female officers usually received safe desk assignments. They performed clerical duties, such as answering telephones and typing reports. Some worked with juveniles or in women's prisons.

After 1972 city police departments began sending women on patrol. *Ladies' Home Journal* wondered how well these women were doing a "man's job." The maga-

A police officer reports from her patrol car. What makes the photo unusual is that it was taken in 1980. The officer is a member of the Berkeley (California) Police Department, which was one of the nation's first police departments to employ women officers in the same capacity as men.

zine's survey and interviews revealed that some departments found females "less aggressive in giving out traffic tickets." In some cases, however, women officers seemed better able than their male colleagues to defuse violent situations. Both males and females made approximately the same number of arrests that resulted in convictions, *LHJ* reported. But biases still existed. Most police officers thought women simply weren't physically or emotionally equipped to handle the demands of police work.

LHJ reported its study in the April 1975 issue. Although the law changed in the 1970s, years would pass before attitudes would also change. By the 1990s, uniformed police-women were commonly seen on patrol in cities across the country. This increased visibility and women's continued success at performing their duties changed the way male officers viewed their female partners. A 1994 study reported that "over 80 percent of the male officers considered women to be accepted members of the law enforcement profession." The study concluded that "the presence of female officers was a 'business-as-usual situation.'"

Oddsmakers had Bobby Riggs an 8–5 prematch favorite over Billie Jean King in their 1973 Battle of the Sexes. But Riggs was no match for King, who trounced him in consecutive sets in front of more than thirty thousand people in the Houston Astrodome and an estimated fifty million television viewers.

Riggs admitted he was a proud male chauvinist pig. Riggs not only believed he was a better tennis player than any woman, he also believed that men were superior to women. To prove it, he challenged Billie Jean King to a tennis match. "You insist that top women players provide a brand of tennis comparable to men's," he said to her. "I challenge you to prove it. I contend that you not only cannot beat a top male player, but that you can't beat me, a tired old man."

At first, the nineteen-year-old King refused to take the bait. Another tennis champion—Australian Margaret Court—did. She lost her match to Riggs on Mother's Day 1973. So badly did Riggs trounce her that the media called the match the Mother's Day Massacre. After his victory, Riggs continued to taunt female athletes and feminists alike. "I want Billie Jean King," he told the media. "I want the women's lib leader."

Billie Jean King was an outspoken advocate for women's sports. In 1971 she became the first female athlete to earn $100,000 in a single year. She complained that women athletes earned much less money than male athletes and that the sports media, in general, gave female athletes little coverage. Yes, she was a women's libber. King decided to take Riggs on, if only to shut him up.

The media hyped the match, calling it the Battle of the Sexes. In 1973 King was physically fit and at the top of her game. She was determined that this would not be another media massacre. While Riggs bragged and posed for magazine and newspaper photographs to promote the match, King was training. She also played along with the jest, posing for publicity shots. But more often, she was on the court, nailing her serve.

On September 30, 1973, millions of Americans—both male and female—turned on their television sets to watch the battle. Bobby Riggs entered the Astrodome in Houston, Texas, in a rickshaw, a type of carriage pulled by people rather than horses. The people Riggs chose to pull the rickshaw were young, beautiful women in tight clothing. He called them his bosom buddies. Not to be outdone, Billie Jean King arrived as if she were Queen Cleopatra of Egypt. She sat on a litter, a red-and-gold draped platform carried on the shoulders of four bare-chested men. Once courtside, Riggs presented his

> ## "It (the match) wasn't about tennis, it was about social change." —Billie Jean King

opponent with a giant Sugar Daddy lollipop, in other words telling her that she was a big sucker and that she was a fool for accepting a challenge she was going to lose. Again, King wasn't to be outdone. She gave him a real live oinking piglet. The show was as entertaining as any episode of *The Bionic Woman*.

After mocking gender stereotypes and each other, the two began the real game. King wore her opponent down, defeating him easily 6–4, 6–3, 6–3. "It wasn't about tennis," King would say later. "It was about social change." A lot was riding on her performance that day, she said, not the least of which was women's self-esteem. "I thought it would set [women] back fifty years if I didn't win that match."

King wasn't a bionic woman, but that made her achievement all the more meaningful. She won because she was physically fit. She won because she didn't crumble under her opponent's taunts. In writing about the match for the *New York Times*, sports editor Neil Amdur said, "Most important perhaps for women everywhere, she convinced skeptics that a female athlete can survive pressure-filled situations and that men are as susceptible to nerves as women."

A year after her match with Riggs, the tennis champion started the Women's Sports Foundation to promote athletic opportunities for females. She also founded *WomenSports* magazine. When *Seventeen* magazine polled its readers in 1975, they named Billie Jean King as the woman they most admired in the world. Her legacy was not in defeating Riggs. She and Riggs remained friends, she said, for years. Her legacy was promoting equity in sports for women. King told women everywhere that it was good to play sports. Her influence on women and society, in general, lasted long after the Battle of the Sexes had faded into television sports history. In 1990 *Life* magazine named her one of the "100 Most Important Americans of the 20th Century."

WOMEN MAKE NEWS, 1983— SALLY RIDE ROCKETS INTO SPACE

Sally Ride had a lot of educational degrees: a BA in English and a BS, MS, and PhD in physics. What Ride didn't have in 1978 was a job. She read an advertisement in her university newspaper. The National Aeronautics and Space Administration (NASA) was seeking applicants for its astronaut training program. Ride applied. NASA received more than eight thousand applications. They selected just thirty-five people. Six of those thirty-five were women. Sally Ride was among them.

The new team of NASA astronauts would fly space shuttle missions. A space shuttle is a winged spacecraft launched into orbit on the back

The world thinks of Sally Ride, shown here in 1983, as the Challenger *astronaut who was the first American woman in space. But her true interest is physics, a field in which she holds a PhD from Stanford University in California. Her website speaks of what is important to her: "My research interests center on the theory of nonlinear beam-wave interactions, primarily connected with free electron lasers and related nonlinear systems."*

of a rocket. A shuttle can orbit Earth for days and then reenter the atmosphere and land safely. Ride was a crew member of the seventh space shuttle mission, Mission STS-7. Her spaceship was called *Challenger*.

Ride would be the first U.S. woman in space. She was a mission specialist, NASA reported. Her task was to operate the shuttle's 50-foot (15-meter) mechanical arm during experiments in space. In press releases, NASA emphasized the STS-7's mission and the experiments the crew would conduct in space. But the news media wanted to know more about Ride. "I didn't come into the space program to be the first woman in space," she told reporters. "I came in to get a chance to fly as soon as I could."

The press didn't give up. "Would she cook while in orbit?" was one of the sillier questions tossed her way. Would she carry makeup and lipstick with her on the flight? "It's too bad that society isn't to the point yet where the country could just send up a woman astronaut and nobody would think twice about it," Ride commented.

Why hadn't a woman flown in space before? Christopher Kraft, a former director of the Johnson Space Center in Houston, provided an answer. "There were no women in the beginning because they didn't meet the qualifications," stated Kraft. The first astronauts of the late 1950s, called the Mercury 7, were all men. The astronauts of the Apollo missions in the 1960s were also men. "They were test pilots," Kraft explained to the media. "They were used to life-and-death situations and put their lives on the line every day."

The first group of female astronauts was admitted to training in 1978. They included, from left, Rhea Seddon, Kathryn Sullivan, Judith Resnik, Sally Ride, Anna Fisher, and Shannon Lucid. The commitment of these women helped pave the way for Ride to be part of the Challenger *crew in 1983 and for Eileen Collins to become the first female shuttle pilot in 1995.*

While that is true, it isn't the whole story. What Kraft failed to tell the press was that in the 1960s the U.S. military didn't allow women to become test pilots. Even so, during this time, NASA had begun a Mercury 13 program for women in addition to its Mercury 7 program for men. The thirteen individuals were called Fellow Lady Astronaut Trainees, or FLATs. The women, all of them pilots, though not test pilots, qualified for the NASA program by undergoing the same grueling physical and psychological tests that the male astronauts took. Many matched or even bested the men's records.

However, under pressure from Congress and then Vice President Lyndon Johnson, NASA ended the program before the women got their chance to suit up and fly.

In the 1960s, society still viewed a woman's place as in the home and not a space capsule. Training an astronaut was very expensive. Some said that if a woman got married and became pregnant, she'd leave the program, wasting the money spent on her training. That was one of the reasons given for dropping the FLAT program. Disappointed, the women fought to resume their training, but NASA held firm. All astronauts had to be test pilots.

By the 1980s, NASA no longer required its astronauts to be pilots. NASA wanted scientists, the best the United States had, male or female. Like Sally Ride, the other seven women selected were also scientists. Judith Resnik held a PhD in electrical engineering. Anna Fisher was a medical doctor, and Rhea Seddon was a surgeon. Kathryn Sullivan had a PhD in geology. Shannon Lucid was a biochemist.

On June 18, 1983, the day that Sally Ride rode *Challenger* into space, Janey Hart sat in the spectators' stands a few miles away from the launch. She was excited for Ride. But she felt disappointment too over what could have been. In the 1960s, she had been one of the FLATs. "It's not true that we've 'come a long way, baby,'" Janey Hart told reporters that day. "We've been there all the time—it's NASA that's come a long way."

"We've been there all the time— it's NASA that's come a long way."
—Janey Hart, 1983

The FLATs weren't the only women celebrating the successful launch of STS-7. In Boston, Massachusetts, World War II veterans of the Women Airforce Service Pilots (WASPs) gathered at a local country club to raise champagne glasses to Dr. Ride. Along a highway in Florida near the launch site, a man sold souvenir T-shirts that read "Ride Sally Ride," a line from the 1960s Wilson Picket song "Mustang Sally." Once the shuttle was in orbit, NASA began broadcasting live images of *Challenger* to Earth. Time described Ride in orbit as "a cheerful, scrub-face young woman," and noted that she had not, after all, carried makeup in her personal kit.

Six days later, *Challenger* landed at Edwards Air Force Base in California. As the astronauts stepped safely on Earth again, an official from NASA congratulated Ride. He handed her a bouquet of carnations.

Barbara Walters's Big Contract

Prior to 1970, a few women had appeared on local television news to read weather forecasts and only a very few women had appeared on television to report on serious issues. Marlene Sanders, Ailene Saarinen, Pauline Frederick, Nancy Dickerson, Barbara Walters, and Liz Trotta were among the very few. But none of them were actual news anchors—the people who introduce, present, or even analyze multiple news stories from various sources or reporters. Walter Cronkite and David Brinkley were two popular news anchors.

Then everything changed. In 1976 Barbara Walters signed a five-year, $5 million contract with ABC television to anchor the prime-time evening news. The salary was astounding at thet time. ABC was paying her to do two jobs, Walters insisted—to coanchor the news with Harry Reasoner and to continue to do feature stories.

Barbara Walters, shown here in 1974, did not officially identify herself with the feminist movement. Yet she opened many doors for women by the career that she forged for herself in the male-dominated field of U.S. network news.

Walters had begun her television journalism career in 1961 as a writer for *The Today Show*, a morning TV newsmagazine. She was the only female writer, and her assignments were fashion reports and celebrity interviews. In time, that changed. She advanced to become a "reporter-at-large," interviewing newsmakers, and eventually cohosting *The Today Show* with Hugh Downs. Her decision to leave that position to coanchor the ABC evening news was a female first.

Walters's career took off in the 1980s. She became a cohost of the popular Sunday evening TV newsmagazine *20/20*. She interviewed world leaders, among them Cuban dictator Fidel Castro. Her television specials featured in-depth interviews with controversial people and with her specialty—Hollywood stars. As her popularity and her ratings increased, so did her salary.

No one had brought flowers for the male astronauts. Ride refused to accept them. The first woman in space just wanted to be treated like a member of the crew. Later, however, in the privacy of a car, she accepted the flowers. Although the first woman in space wanted to be treated no differently from any other astronaut, she became a heroine to many young girls in the United States. Like Ride, they loved science and space and the thrill of adventure.

INTO THE EIGHTIES

By the 1980s, television images of women were changing. *The Mary Tyler Moore Show* had gone off the air after an impressive run of seven seasons. Jaimie "The Bionic Woman" Sommers had left her top-secret government job. She had told her supervisor she needed time to have a life of her own. *Charlie's Angels* was no longer soaring in the television ratings, and the network canceled the show.

Male characters had dominated the television airwaves in the 1970s. In 1973, 74 percent of the characters on television were male. In the 1980s, however, women gained ground, despite the departure of Mary Richards, Jaimie Sommers, and the Angels. New programs with new fictional female characters premiered.

Cagney and Lacey was a police drama about two female detectives. Unlike the Angels of the 1970s, Cagney and Lacey did not appear in bikinis. They were street smart rather

Tyne Daly (left) *and Sharon Gless* (right) *are shown here on the set of* Cagney and Lacey *in the mid-1980s. The popular show was less a crime drama than a show about the real-life struggles and heartaches of two women who happened to work as police officers.*

than sexy. They certainly were not angelic in their behavior. They argued, they made mistakes, and they expressed their frustrations. Mary Beth Lacey was married, a working mom who made tuna casseroles for her family. At times, she struggled to keep her career and her home life in balance. Chris Cagney was single. She was ambitious and could be bossy and acid-tongued to those who challenged her authority. Often the challenge came from her fellow male police officers, who resented "broads" on the force. But these characters also had a sense of humor and a sense of loyalty to each other. They were good at their jobs. In many ways, the characters were realistic rather than idealistic portrayals of women.

Other programs, too, featured strong females in leading roles. *Kate and Allie* was a comedy about two divorced women raising their children. *Designing Women* explored the ups and downs of four women running their own interior design business. In dramas, women's roles included attorneys, detectives, and waitresses. *Murder, She Wrote* featured a woman mystery writer who solves crimes.

Women had always had a presence in television, said Harvey Shepard of the CBS Television Network. In the past, however, studios cast women in comedies or as sex symbols. "They had to be in non-threatening roles," said Shepard. Networks

Kate and Allie, *the cast of which is shown here, dealt with practical problems faced by divorced women with children. During the show's 1984–1989 run, it also faced the larger issue of gender roles. At this time, many American women were struggling with being a loving wife and mother as well as a competent professional who deserved equality at work.*

Angela Lansbury, shown here during a 1985 episode of Murder, She Wrote, *played a middle-aged widowed mystery writer amateur detective. The show, which debuted in 1984 and ran for twelve years, became television's longest-running mystery series. It went one step beyond* Cagney and Lacey *in proving that youth and sex appeal were not necessary for a successful TV series.*

feared that forceful women would turn off viewers, and without viewers, the networks couldn't sell ads during the programs. By the mid-1980s, however, television polls proved to producers that Americans were eager for programs that featured strong female characters. The real-life accomplishments of women, such as Sally Ride and Billie Jean King, in part, spurred the change. Activist groups such as NOW also pressured networks to rethink the roles of women. The viewers themselves demanded change. When CBS cancelled *Cagney and Lacey*, viewers launched a letter-writing campaign demanding the network continue the program. The network did.

"There is nothing coincidental about this trend," Shepard told a reporter for the *New York Times* in the fall of 1984. "We are finding that there is a growing acceptance of the more liberated role of women. Our schedule reflects that."

Chapter Three

From Denial to Indulgence—
The Body Obsession

Kate Moss poses for Calvin Klein's male fragrance Obsession in 1995.

You run a $1.5 billion business, and it boils down to whether some chicks look good in their uniform. If you have fat stewardesses, people aren't going to fly with you.

—*airline executive, quoted in the* New York Times, *March 4, 1972*

Professor Mary K. Bentley was on a mission.

One afternoon in the 1990s, armed with a tape measure, she entered a department store determined to record the body proportions of a few female mannequins. The sales clerk thought her behavior was odd and explained she couldn't disturb the displays. She was writing a book on adolescent girls, Bentley explained, but the clerk called the manager. He, in turn, sent her to the store's corporate offices. Eventually, the corporate office put her in touch with the man who was in charge of creating the mannequin displays. From him, she got the measurements: bust—32 inches (81 centimeters); waist—23 inches (58 cm); hips—31 inches (79 cm).

She measured another mannequin, which was much the same, give or take an inch. "Both [mannequins] had 18-inch [46 cm] thighs and upper arms of less than 10 inches [25 cm]," Bentley later wrote. "A mannequin is by definition a life-sized model of the human body, used to fit or display clothes. If the forms he [the display manager] measured were real bodies, there would be very little life in them."

When compared to international sizing charts, the numbers were shockingly short of the typical American woman's size in the 1990s. That woman generally had about a 38-inch (97 cm) bust, a 29- to 31-inch (74 to 79 cm) waist, and 39- to 40-inch (99 to 102 cm) hips. Were American women fat? Or were the department store mannequins on the verge of starvation?

The man who dressed mannequins for a living explained. Mannequin bodies changed over the years, depending on the

A fashion designer stands among his mannequins in 1972. As unrealistically slender-waisted as these forms are, they are closer to a woman's natural body than many others.

clothing styles. In the 1950s, for example, the mannequins had large breasts and hips but small, cinched waists to promote the styles of the time. In the late 1960s and 1970s, the flat-chested, little-girl look became more popular, and so the mannequins lost weight (or rather plaster). At the time Bentley was doing her research, the mannequin dressers told her, "The waif-like heroin addict is the look that dominates most of the young women's displays."

Bentley got the idea of measuring the mannequins after overhearing two thirteen-year-old girls talking in the store. They were admiring a dress on a mannequin. One girl said she loved it, but she'd have to lose 40 pounds (18 kilograms) to wear it. The friend suggested that if she didn't eat for a few days, it might work.

Mannequins are a type of three-dimensional advertisement. They sell clothing and jewelry. But they also sell something else, said Bentley. They sell an image of what a girl's body should be. But the image, at least this mannequin image, was not just unrealistic, it was unhealthy.

Source: *Shape Magazine*

©Daryl Cagle: http://www.cagle.com/art

The department store Saks Fifth Avenue introduced a new mannequin in 1995 as the "ideal woman of the '90s." As shown in this cartoon, the mannequin was 6 feet (183 cm) tall and wore a size 6 dress. The average woman at that time was 5 feet 4 inches (162 cm) tall and wore a size 10–12 dress.

The Mademoiselle Fantasy

According to the U.S. Labor Bureau, women represented 40 percent of the total labor force in 1975. However, flipping through the pages of *Mademoiselle* that same year suggests the Labor Bureau had it all wrong. The images of women in the magazine's photographs and ads do not show women working. Instead, the women dance in meadows of wildflowers. They ride bikes. They walk dogs. They lie on the floor in yellow bikinis and browse through travel brochures. They look at themselves in mirrors. They put on lipstick, curl their hair, apply suntan lotion, and suck flavored ice sticks. They look at themselves in mirrors. They hold roses, fishing rods, and basketballs, but they don't garden, gut a fish, or shoot a basket. They look at themselves in mirrors.

The waiflike look of the 1990s was cultivated by models such as Kate Moss, shown here in 1993. Models enhanced their gaunt look with makeup to hollow the cheeks and enlarge the eyes. Minimalist clothing allowed bone structures to show. Though the hazards of smoking were documented fact by the mid-1990s, a cigarette completes Moss's less-than-healthy look.

Mademoiselle's readers were primarily young women in their teens and twenties. The magazine's models were young, white, and thin. They had no visible wrinkles, crooked teeth, or dandruff. They were seemingly perfect, but they were as much a fantasy as the gynoids in *The Stepford Wives.* Graphic artists routinely touch up images of men and women in magazines. That is, they erase wrinkles, soften sharp jawlines, and lighten dark circles under the eyes. They can trim inches off hips, calves, or upper arms. Said a former art director for *Life* magazine, "No picture of a woman goes unretouched."

But why alter the images at all? Is it because the United States loves youth and beauty? Not quite, says author Naomi Wolf. The fantasy is less about beauty and lifestyle and more about money. "The advertisers who make mass marketing possible," said Wolf, "depend on making women feel bad enough about their faces and bodies to spend more." So for the average woman to resemble the image of a model, she's required to purchase a lot of beauty materials, including glossy lipsticks, blush, antiwrinkle creams, and diet products that supposedly reduce the size of buttocks and abdomens. Magazines make their profits from advertisements for these products.

Good-Bye, Thunder Thighs

Women's bodies were big advertising business throughout the twentieth century. In the 1970s, the fashion trend was thinness. "How Do You Measure Up?" *Mademoiselle* asked its readers in a feature story on dieting. The photograph illustrating the story showed a woman's bare waist around which she tugged a measuring tape. Her waist was smaller than 25 inches (63 cm).

The majority of American women believed they didn't measure up to the standards presented in popular magazines through ads and articles. In a 1984 article, *Glamour* magazine reported the results of a survey it conducted among its readers. Approximately thirty-three thousand women, ranging in age from nineteen to thirty-five, responded. About 75 percent of these women admitted that they thought they were fat. Were they overweight? Not necessarily. *Glamour* titled its article "Feeling Fat in a Thin Society," stating that even women who weren't overweight thought they were. Even underweight women, the magazine reported, had a goal of "losing 10–15 pounds [4.5 to 7 kg]." The women rated losing weight as a more important goal than falling in love.

Thunder thighs, saddlebags, and love handles—these are phrases American society uses to describe extra weight on a person's legs, hips, or waist. In a thinness-obsessed society, models on the cover of magazines and in advertisements are willowy and flat chested. Their splayed legs are coltishly slender. Books with titles such as *Thin*

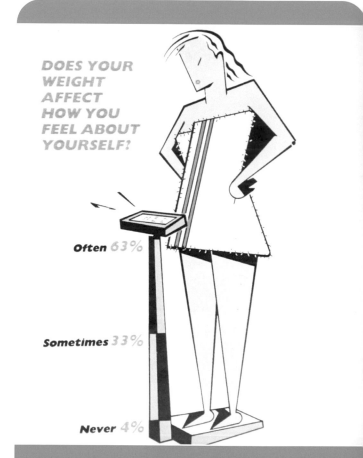

DOES YOUR WEIGHT AFFECT HOW YOU FEEL ABOUT YOURSELF?

Often 63%

Sometimes 33%

Never 4%

Glamour's 1984 survey found that 96 percent of all women felt that their self-esteem was affected by their weight.

Thighs in Thirty Days become best sellers.

The United States in the last quarter of the twentieth century was a thinness-obsessed society. While men, too, might have had "spare tires" of fat around their waists, the media placed more emphasis on the ideal woman as slender. The thin-is-in trend *Glamour* reported in the 1980s continued into the 1990s. "The average model, dancer, or actress is thinner than 95 percent of the female population," wrote Naomi Wolf in 1991. Kate Moss, a popular model of the early 1990s, stood 5 feet 7 inches (170 cm) tall and weighed approximately 100 pounds (45 kg).

Advertisers pressured women to purchase their products by promoting guilt and fear of fat. This advertisement for Tombstone Light Pizza appeared in the 1995 issue of *Glamour*, a magazine read mostly by young women:

> He eats a brownie . . . You eat a rice cake.
> He eats a juicy burger . . . You eat a low fat entrée.
> He eats a pizza . . . YOU eat a pizza.
> Finally, life is fair.

Ladies' Home Journal magazine also has a female readership, generally older than that of *Glamour*. Many *LHJ* readers are married with children. In one issue, a full-page advertisement for Ayds Reducing Plan told the story of an overweight housewife and mother. Her

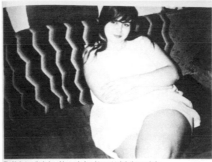

The inspiring stories in the ads for Ayds weight-loss candy (above) appealed to many people in the 1970s. They were attracted to the idea that someone could lose weight easily by eating something normally associated with gaining weight. They also were drawn to the way the ads created a Cinderella-like transformation of a lonely woman into a confident beauty.

husband nagged her to lose weight. Her son called her a hippopotamus, and that hurt, she said. The woman solved her weight problem, however, by eating Ayds candies. Eat candy to lose weight? It sounded too good to be true! And yet the ad was persuasive. It showed two photographs of the same woman, one before she started the Ayds plan at 160 pounds (72 kg) and one after at 112 pounds (50 kg).

Ayds claimed the candy suppressed the appetite so a person ate less. Ayds's before-and-after advertisements appeared in numerous periodicals in the 1970s and 1980s, and the candy was among the top-selling diet products of those decades.

Despite the before-and-after photographs and testimony from women who used Ayds candies, the American Medical Association was skeptical that any chemical dietary aid was an effective way to lose weight. Despite the candy packaging, the active ingredient in Ayds was indeed a chemical, with a very long name: phenylpropanolamine (PPA).

The consequences of women's obsession with diet and weight became serious, even life threatening. Eating disorders such as anorexia nervosa and bulimia made headlines. Anorexia is an extreme fear of becoming overweight, leading to extreme dieting, to the point of endangering health. Popular musician Karen Carpenter made headlines when she collapsed onstage during a performance in Las Vegas, Nevada. Rushed to the hospital, she weighed in at 80 pounds (36 kg). The doctors determined that she was severely underweight. Carpenter didn't think so. She purposely starved herself, took diet pills, and induced vomiting so that she would never again be "chubby." Her near-death experience helped her to seek medical and psychiatric treatment for anorexia. But

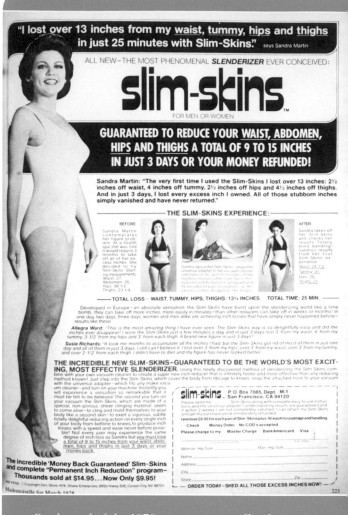

By the end of the 1970s, women were offered extreme alternatives to dieting via advertising. Soon the Federal Trade Commission challenged the growing weight loss industry and attempted to put a stop to its false claims such as in the ad above.

in 1983, at the age of thirty-three, Karen Carpenter died from the disease.

Bulimia is an eating disorder characterized by overeating and then purging through laxatives or self-induced vomiting before the body can absorb essential nutrients. Like anorexia, bulimia is associated in part with depression and anxiety about weight.

Throughout the 1970s and 1980s, health-care experts increasingly emphasized the dangers of eating disorders. "I think weight obsession may be the most prevalent form of emotional disorder among women today," stated Dr. Susan Wooley in a *New York Times* article. "We know that between 20 and 30 percent of female college students engage in some kind of binge-purge behavior where they gorge themselves on as many as 10,000 calories at a time (the equivalent of five 10-inch [25 cm] cheese pizzas and two 8-inch [20 cm] chocolate layer cakes) and then either vomit or take laxatives."

Singer and musician Karen Carpenter, a member of the musical duo the Carpenters, is shown here on a 1970 episode of The Ed Sullivan Show. *Carpenter suffered from anorexia, a relatively unknown disease at the time. She had planned to go public with her battle once she had the illness under control, but she died of the disease at the age of thirty-three.*

Meanwhile, the images of women in the popular media—women's magazines, in particular—emphasized thinness as the ideal female body shape. Articles and advertising text reinforced the idea that indulging in food was a loss of self-control. *Pizza Without Guilt* was a Weight Watchers' advertising promise. "What you do in the dark is nobody else's business," stated Milky Way candy's ad.

A woman didn't even have to open a magazine to get the message. It appeared again and again in bold headlines on the covers: "Hollywood Diet—How the Stars Stay Slim," "I Love My New Thighs," "Get the Body You Really Want," "Tighten Your Butt." Even products that weren't promoting diet plans, exercise routines, or diet foods emphasized a woman's size. "Have you lost weight?" asks a man whose hands are on a woman's waist. "No," she answers, "I just found Berkshire pantyhose." The model in the photograph is thin. She wears a backless dress. The reader does not have to look closely to see her shoulder blades and the nodules of her spine. The fact that the man is holding her, entranced, suggests that thin women find love.

A study in the early 1990s indicated that the magazines most frequently read by women contained ten times the number of advertisements and articles on weight and dieting than the magazines read by men. Men, too, suffered from anorexia and bulimia. However, ten times as many women suffered as did men. It was no coincidence, said researchers, that the ratio of eating disorders in women and men was the same as the ratio of emphasis on weight and dieting in the popular magazines. By the end of the century, between 90 and 95 percent of those who suffered from eating disorders were women.

Men, too, suffered from anorexia and bulimia. However, ten times as many women suffered as did men.

The Orange-Peel Skin Panic

The term *cellulite* first came into popular use in European spas and beauty salons. In the United States in 1973, the owner of a New York beauty spa published a book titled *Cellulite: Those Lumps, Bumps, and Bulges You Couldn't Lose Before*. Author Nicole Ronsard described cellulite as "fat gone wrong." Those little dimples of fat on a female's body were a symptom of toxins, or poisons, in a woman's body. Her intestines, liver, and kidneys had failed to eliminate these toxins. The result? Orange-peel skin—natural on fruit, unnatural and ugly on a woman's buttocks.

Orange-peel skin wasn't a medical condition, as Ronsard suggested, however. Biologist Marci Greenwood told *Time* magazine that cellulite was simply fat caused by the loss of skin elasticity. Being overweight didn't cause cellulite, and so dieting couldn't cure it.

Women Make News, 1982—The Drum Majorette of Monongahela

Peggy Ward had skipped meals and taken diet pills. She often felt weak and dizzy as a result, but unless she shed 4 more pounds (1.8 kg), she could not march with her high school band. Peggy was a drum majorette. She had already lost 8 pounds (3.6 kg) over the past four weeks. Her family doctor stated that Peggy's weight of 130 pounds (59 kg) was perfectly normal for her age and height, which was 5 feet 4 inches (163 cm). He disapproved of her taking diet pills. They could lead to more serious health issues, he said.

In October 1982, majorette Peggy Ward (left) was not allowed to march with the Ringgold High School band at halftime of a football game because she weighed 1.5 pounds (0.7 kg) more than the 126-pound (57 kg) limit set by a doctor as the ideal weight for her height. The message to young teens was loud and clear: every additional pound counts against you.

Despite her doctor's insistence that Peggy's weight was normal, both the band director and the school principal refused to change the decision. Peggy would not march on the football field until she lost those additional pounds. It was a matter of looking good, the principal told a news reporter. It was a matter of discipline, said the band director. Both school officials implied that Peggy didn't care enough about her appearance to shed the extra weight. Classmates and even the adult fans in the bleachers during the football games jeered at those girls on the cheerleading squad considered fat, so why should band members be exempt?

Peggy felt it was "unfair" to be judged by her appearance rather than her ability as a majorette. But Peggy gave in to the pressure, and she kept dieting. On game day, the school nurse weighed Peggy. She had lost more weight, but not enough. She was still 1.5 pounds (0.7 kg) over the limit. She did not march.

Peggy's school in Monongahela, Pennsylvania, was not the only high school in the country that set weight restrictions for its female baton twirlers. According to the National Federation of State High School Associations, in the 1980s, many schools had similar restrictions.

Lack of exercise didn't cause it, so exercising would not smooth out the dimples. Cellulite, said Greenwood, was simply a matter of body type and aging. "Body type, like hair color and the distance between your eyes, is inherited, and the same is true for the distance between your fatty deposits."

American women seemed not to pay attention to medical opinions. That's not really so surprising. If something is hereditary, you can't do much about it. Instead, women young and old bought Ronsard's book by the hundreds of thousands. The orange-peel skin panic had begun. Soon after, ways to remove cellulite became big business. Other publishers produced books on the treatment of the dreaded dimples. Cosmetic companies created new products—lotions, gels, herbal pills, body wraps, and muscle stimulators to rub away, melt away, or break down the toxins.

Did the lotions and body wraps work? No, said the Federal Trade Commission (FTC), a government agency that protects consumers. In 1986 the FTC stated that rubbing, wrapping, or scrubbing would not remove cellulite, nor would vitamins or dieting. Even thin people, both men and women, have dimpled fat deposits. Surely the muscle stimulators would do the trick? No, again, said the FTC. Such machines, costing hundreds of dollars, could damage the body. Relax-A-Cizor was a kind

The Relaxacizor claimed to reduce hips, waistline, abdomen and thighs "without physical effort" through electrical stimulation of the muscles. What it actually did was deliver electrical shocks through its contact pads. Among the potential side effects were abnormal heart rhythms, miscarriages, and worsening of hernias, ulcers, and epilepsy. For these reasons, the FTC eventually banned the sale of the product.

of padding a person strapped onto the body. Supposedly, wires within the padding gave little electric shocks to the body, eliminating fat. A person could wear this padding while watching TV, reading a book, or even sleeping and lose those troublesome lumps and bumps. However, the FTC determined that the Relax-A-Cizor had caused injury in people who had used it, including hernias, ulcers, and varicose veins. The agency ordered the product off the market.

One treatment, however, did work: exercising. Although exercising does not eliminate cellulite, toning the muscles reduces the appearance of cellulite. Exercising is hard work and takes time. American women prefer a quicker fix, reported *Newsweek*. "They find the idea of a magic body potion irresistible, and they're willing to pay whatever it costs."

The editor of *Allure* magazine agrees. "Even though the creams don't do what's promised," said Linda Wells, "women go against their common sense and buy them anyway. I thought women were smarter than that."

Changing the Mirror Image

"Advertising doesn't cause eating problems," said Jean Kilbourne, who has studied the media's influence on women. But she added, "Advertising does promote abusive and abnormal attitudes about eating, drinking and thinness."

Instead of changing her body's size and shape, Carol Normandi changed the way she viewed herself in the mirror. She accepted a more realistic body image, one based on her age and heredity rather than

Carol Emery Normandi and Laurelee Roark are the cofounders of Beyond Hunger. This organization acknowledges the ever-increasing problem that obsession about weight and eating is causing women—especially young girls. The Council on Size and Weight Discrimination reports that young girls are more afraid of becoming fat than they are of nuclear war, cancer, or losing their parents. By 1982, 65 percent of eleven-year-olds felt that they were too fat.

models and magazine fantasies. Once she stopped hating her body, she could give up dieting. She gained two dress sizes. But that was OK, she said. "I was aspiring to the body of a male adolescent instead of a healthy, full-grown, developed female." Normandi later founded Beyond Hunger, a support group for women to cope with body images.

The Fat Vacuum and the Tummy Tuck

Body contouring, or body sculpting—that's the way some plastic surgeons describe the liposuction procedure. It sounds almost like creating a statue, a work of art. But the actual liposuction procedure is much less lovely.

To research an article for *Mademoiselle* in 1988, journalist Jill Neimark got permission to witness a liposuction procedure on a woman's thigh. The plastic surgeon sliced the skin of the thigh and inserted a flexible tube called a cannula. The cannula acts like a vacuum hose. "What comes next is almost unbelievably violent," wrote Neimark. The surgeon "begins to thrust the cannula in and out, as rapid as a piston, breaking through thick nets of fat, nerves and tissues in her leg." The vacuum can suck up to 2 quarts (2,000 milliliters) of tissue and blood from the body. "Any more," reported Neimark, "would put (the patient) at risk for massive infection. . . ." Then the surgeon stitches the incisions.

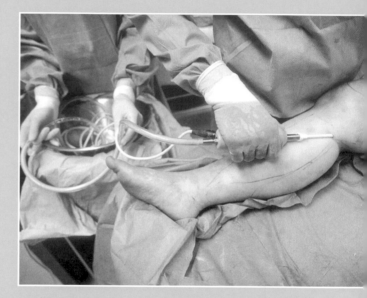

In the 1980s, many U.S. surgeons began to experiment with liposuction, the removal of fat by vacuum suction. The procedure can be applied to thighs as shown above, as well as to buttocks, neck, backs of the arms and abdomen.

Abdominoplasty is the medical term for a "tummy tuck." The majority of patients who undergo abdominoplasty are women. This major surgery requires general anesthesia. The surgeon slices open the stomach below the navel from hip to hip. The surgeon then removes a triangular section of skin and fat. Next, the surgeon cuts "a pocket" under the skin from above the navel up to the ribs. Loosened from the abdominal wall, this flap of skin is then stretched downward and sewn to the lower incision.

Tummy tucks and liposuctions are considered elective surgeries. That means they are not medically necessary to save a life or cure an illness. The media's body obsession in the last quarter of the twentieth century significantly increased the practice of elective plastic surgery. In addition to tucking tummies and sucking fat, surgeons sculpt chins; bob noses; lift eyelids, foreheads, and breasts; transplant hair; and tighten and whiten skin.

In 1992 approximately 50 million Americans—mostly women— were on some kind of diet. Diet books were on the best-seller list. Membership in weight-loss support organizations, such as Weight Watchers and Jenny Craig, soared. Meanwhile, a small but growing number of women, such as Carol Normandi, had begun to fight fat differently. They threw away the diet books and pills and prepackaged foods. Some even smashed their bathroom scales. An antidiet movement had taken root and was spreading, reported the *New York Times* in 1992.

Organizations such as Fat Underground, the Fat Liberation Front, and the Council on Size and Weight Discrimination began campaigns to promote what they called size acceptance. The idea was simple. Instead of changing bodies, change minds. They demanded to know who said thin was in. Who said men fall in love only with thin women? Talk back to the visual images in popular culture, they urged women. You can be beautiful at any size.

Among the leaders of the antidiet movement were two therapists, Jane Hirschmann and Carol Munter. They published a book titled *Overcoming Overeating*. Women who hate their bodies, they wrote, do so because they believe two things. First, they believe there is "an 'ideal' body and theirs is far from it." Second, they believe "eating is something that must be controlled." Those ideas are wrong, the authors insisted.

Women learned these ideas, they said, from the popular media that surrounded them with messages that thin was beautiful and healthy, and overindulging in food was a loss of self-control.

At 5 feet 7 inches tall (170 cm) weighing 214 pounds (96 kg), Jean Nidetch was an overweight housewife who enlisted her friends to help her stay on a diet. She hit upon a plan of healthy eating and exercise that worked and incorporated Weight Watchers *in 1963. By 1968 the organization had franchises across the United States.*

Diets don't work, the authors stated. A 1992 study from the National Institutes of Health showed that within a year of stopping a diet, most dieters gained back one-third to two-thirds of the weight they had lost. Within five years, they had regained "nearly all" of the lost weight.

The first step in size acceptance, stated Hirschmann and Munter, was buying a full-length mirror and looking at yourself. For women obsessed with body weight, a mirror can be an enemy, but "mirror work" was an activity the authors recommended. Learning to see the real person in the mirror rather than a media image would take time and practice. The second and third steps were throwing out the bathroom scale and cleaning out the closet of clothes that were too small and didn't fit. The message was simple: learn to accept yourself instead of punishing yourself.

> Learning to see the real person in the mirror rather than a media image would take time and practice.

"I see my body in the mirror now and am getting better each day at being kind to myself," wrote one woman to the authors. "I used to try not to look because I knew I wouldn't see that *Sports Illustrated* swimsuit model figure that I knew I should have."

Who Controls a Woman's Body?

Jane Roe wasn't her real name. It was an alias to protect her privacy. In 1969 she was in her early twenties, married, and expecting a baby—a baby she neither wanted nor could afford to raise. In Texas where Jane Roe lived, abortion was against the law unless the mother's life was in danger. Roe could travel to another state that allowed abortions, but she could not afford this. She decided to have her baby and give it up for adoption. But Jane Roe's story did not end with that decision.

Attorneys Sarah Weddington (left) and Linda Coffee (right) argued the policy-making Roe v. Wade *abortion case before the U.S. Supreme Court in 1973. Their victory made abortion legal in the United States. Coffee was only twenty-six at the time and is thought to be the youngest person to have ever argued a case before the Supreme Court.*

Attorneys Sarah Weddington and Linda Coffee met with Jane Roe to discuss her case. Roe worked as a waitress, but she would lose her job once her pregnancy became advanced. "She could barely support herself, much less a child," said Weddington. "I told her about our ultimate goal: to make abortion a woman's choice and a safe medical procedure."

Weddington and Coffee challenged the Texas abortion law, eventually arguing the case before the U.S. Supreme Court. The Fourteenth Amendment to the Constitution guaranteed a person's right to personal privacy. Personal privacy, the attorneys argued, included a woman's body. A woman's choice to carry or to terminate a pregnancy was a private decision and not one that government should make or force upon women. The 1973 case became known as *Roe v. Wade*. Wade was the last name of the district attorney in Texas who defended the existing state law banning abortion.

When she appeared before the Texas Supreme Court, Weddington emphasized that she was not there to advocate, or support, abortion. "We do not ask this court to rule that abortion is good or desirable in any particular situation. We are here to advocate that the decision as to whether or not a particular woman will continue to carry or terminate a pregnancy is a decision that should be made by that woman.

The Other Body Odor

A 1974 advertisement for Pursettes tampons used a four-panel cartoon to tell the humiliating story of a blonde cheerleader. Her purse spills onto the gym floor, scattering its contents. The cheerleader scurries to pick up a tampon before anyone, especially the male basketball players, can learn "her secret." A second cheerleader introduces her to Pursettes. They fit neatly in a compact, she explains, because they have no bulky applicator. "Pursettes save you all sorts of embarrassments," reads the text. Is menstruation something to be ashamed of? The ad suggests it is. Hiding tampons in a purse was not a girl's only worry, however. "The trickiest problem a girl has isn't under her pretty little arms," an advertisement for Pristeen read. It was between her legs. Pristeen was a feminine deodorant spray. It was "essential to your cleanliness," the text read. "And to your peace of mind about being a girl."

Feminine body odor, like menstruation, is a natural body function caused by hormones. Washing with soap is all that is needed in response. Yet, rather than assure a young woman of this normal, healthy state of being, the advertisements of the 1970s played on her fear of embarrassment.

That such an advertisement existed, however, suggests something else about teenage girls of the 1970s and 1980s: they were becoming more sexually active. Had the women's liberation movement of the 1970s triggered this phenomenon? Surely the birth control pill, which had become available in the 1960s, helped to erase the fear of pregnancy for many sexually active women. Or had young women always experienced and experimented with such relationships but not talked about them so openly? One thing had changed in the last quarter of the twentieth century—discussions of women's bodies, including menstruation, in popular media were more common than in previous decades.

In the first decades of the twentieth century, ads for feminine hygiene products were almost non-existent. Early ads were very discreet and somewhat medically oriented. But by the 1970s, advertisers were dealing directly with the subject, such as in the above ad for tampons aimed at teenagers.

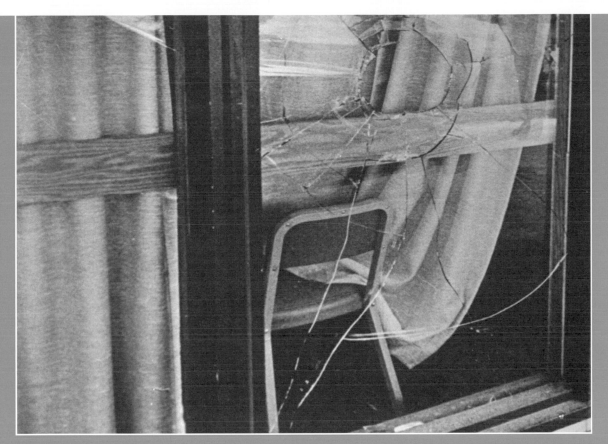

Extreme antiabortion advocates expressed their views by bombing abortion clinics or targeting doctors who performed the procedure. The photo shows the results of a 1978 shoot-up and fire bombing of an Appleton, Wisconsin, abortion clinic owned by feminist and pro-choice advocate Maggi Gage.

And that, in fact, she has a constitutional right to make that decision for herself."

The U.S. Supreme Court did not agree, but in 1973, the majority ruled in favor of Jane Roe by a vote of 7–2. In doing so, the U.S. Supreme Court made abortion within the first three months of a pregnancy legal not only in Texas but in every state.

Roe v. Wade divided the country. The decision was about more than a woman's personal privacy. It touched upon the role of government in a woman's life and the very definition of life. A woman's decision whether to have or not have a baby is not something the government should make, stated Weddington. "It's for an individual woman to make."

Millions of Americans did not support the decision. They believed that life begins at conception and abortion causes the death of a living human being. They labeled themselves pro-lifers. On the other hand, millions of Americans did support the decision. They called themselves pro-choicers. Even many of those who disapproved of abortion believed it should be a woman's legal right to choose whether to have one. Forbidding abortion could condemn many

How would you like the police to investigate your miscarriage?

So-called "pro-lifers" think nothing of invading women's privacy and jeopardizing their health. Their national campaign of violence and intimidation attracts plenty of media attention.

But the outrages they commit now are nothing compared to what would happen if they win.

Their Human Life Amendment to the Constitution treats the fetus as an independent human being from the very instant of fertilization. Abortion would be called murder under all circumstances. So would many effective birth control methods. And every miscarriage could be suspect.

While some anti-choice activists declare that only health professionals who assist with an abortion should be charged with murder, countless women could be caught up in police investigations and prosecutions even if they are never arraigned.

If the right to choose abortion is limited or eliminated, women who can afford to travel could probably evade the law.

Poor women and teenagers with no resources would be forced to induce their own abortions or subject themselves to an illicit, dangerous back-alley procedure.

And thousands of them would be brutalized, maimed and killed.

How do we know what will happen if the extremists win? Because that's the way it was before abortion was made legal and safe in 1973. The choice they present isn't whether abortion should be stopped.

Prohibition never worked.

The choice is privacy...or punishment. Safety for women...or terrible danger.

It's really not a choice we need to make again.

Make time to save your right to choose. Before the so-called "pro-lifers" start making your choices for you.

Take action! To support Planned Parenthood's Campaign to Keep Abortion Safe and Legal, please mail your contribution to PPFA, 810 Seventh Avenue, New York, New York 10019-5818.

Don't wait until women are dying again.

Planned Parenthood® Federation of America

Your body is a battleground

March on Washington
Sunday, April 9, 1989

Support Legal Abortion
Birth Control
and Women's Rights

On April 26 the Supreme Court will hear a case which the Bush Administration hopes will overturn the Roe vs. Wade decision, which established basic abortion rights. Join thousands of women and men in Washington D.C. on April 9. We will show that the majority of Americans support a woman's right to choose.

Washington: Assemble at the Ellipse between the Washington Monument and the White House at 10 am; Rally at the Capitol at 1:30.

Planned Parenthood released ads to support pro-choice policy. The 1980 ad at left shows male police officers arriving at a woman's home to investigate her reproductive activities. Ads such as the one at right from 1989 appealed to women to attend a March on Washington that year to show support for legal abortion, birth control, and women's rights in general.

women and their children to poverty, some said. Furthermore, without legal and safe abortions, women would seek illegal and often unsafe abortions that could kill them. Pro-life and pro-choice groups would continue the debate over when life began and who controlled a woman's body through the end of the century. Many Christian churches disapproved of abortion. The debate extended beyond religion into local and national politics. Whether a candidate for public office held pro-life or pro-choice views could influence the election outcome. The debate became violent at times. Bombs exploded in abortion clinics, killing patients and caregivers.

Jane Roe never had an abortion. As planned, she gave birth and then gave the baby girl up for adoption. For many years, Roe remained a pro-choice activist, volunteering at Planned Parenthood clinics. Eventually, however, she changed her beliefs. In the 1990s, Roe began speaking with pro-life groups. Abortion was terminating a life, she believed. Her conversion from the pro-choice to pro-life viewpoint gave hope to millions of Americans determined to overturn the Supreme Court decision. The passionate debate over a woman's right to choose whether to carry or terminate a pregnancy continued through the end of the century.

The Media's Focus on Female Sexuality

Dazzle him! Take his breath away! Put him under your spell! The right prom dress apparently could do just that, or so teen magazines such as *Young Miss* (*YM*) and *Seventeen* stated. The "right" prom dress might be backless one year and strapless the next. It might be short, black, and hip-hugging tight. Then again, it might be long, pink, and flouncy. Whatever the latest style, however, the message was much the same: how a girl dressed was important in attracting the opposite sex.

All advertisements have a subtext, or an underlying message. The subtext is never a direct statement. Rather, it is implied or suggested through words or other symbols, including images, music, and special effects. The subtext of many advertisements from the 1970s through the 1990s suggested that female sexuality was a way to achieve whatever a woman wanted. And what a woman really wanted, the subtexts often implied, was a romantic relationship with a man. "Remember what they say, Gentlemen prefer Hanes" was the text of a 1980s advertisement for women's stockings. The image that accompanied the text suggested "they" were men. In one Hanes image, a man and a woman enter a theater. The woman is wearing a long evening dress. The man's attention, however, is focused on another woman sitting in a chair. She is wearing a short skirt revealing her long, slim legs. In another Hanes image, a man stares at a flight attendant who is wearing a miniskirt.

The early Hanes ads assumed that all women would be thrilled to have men staring at their legs. As the feminist movement progressed, advertisers had to rethink such assumptions and readjust their ads.

The subtexts of these advertisements implied that men viewed women as sexual objects. They didn't necessarily prefer the Hanes brand over any other kind, but they sure liked ogling women's legs.

Using sex appeal to sell products was not new in the last three decades of the twentieth century. What was new—or at least what was changing—was society's attitude toward female sexuality. Popular culture reflected this change of attitude in a variety of ways. In the 1970s, teen magazines *YM* and *Seventeen* published articles on fashion and romance. Discussion of female sexuality focused on subjects such as flirting, kissing, and how to say no to a boyfriend who pressures a girl into going "further" than kissing or touching. Innocence, these magazines implied, was a female quality that guys couldn't resist.

By the 1980s, sexiness had replaced innocence as a desired female characteristic. The magazines described hair styles and bathing suits as "sexy" and shades of nail polish as "passionate." The articles continued to coach female readers on ways to attract, hold, and please men, and saying "no" to sexual advances seemed less important an issue. "A lot of girls don't talk to their parents, and it has traditionally been the role of *Seventeen* to answer questions our readers are too embarrassed to talk to Mom about," said Caroline Miller, editor-in-chief of the popular magazine. Judging by the selection of articles in the magazine, beginning in the 1980s, those embarrassing questions increasingly were about female sexuality. In 1982 *Seventeen* began publishing a new monthly column titled Sex and Your Body. No one magazine or editor stated explicitly that adolescent girls should have sexual experiences. But the increased attention to and discussion of sexuality in the

These teen magazines each represent their respective decades well. At left, an issue from 1974 shows a freckled-face girl with a simple hairdo and features articles on how to look pretty for prom night or how to bounce back from a breakup. The 1982 cover in the center still shows a few freckles to indicate youth, but the model has more makeup and a more sophisticated hairstyle. The featured article for the back-to-school issue is "Sex and Your Body." Moving into the 1990s, YM features a glamourous actress as cover girl and offers articles such as "Lies Guys Tell for Sex" and "The Older Guy—Do You Dare Date Him?"

pages of teen magazines suggested that adolescent girls were sexually active . . . or soon would be.

By the 1990s, discussion of sexual activity was more blatant. In a June 1994 *Seventeen* article on virginity, an author wrote, "If you don't let somebody pressure you into having sex, why should you let somebody else pressure you into not having sex?" Statements like these illustrated a shift in attitude: from men viewing women as sexual objects to a discussion of women as sexual beings with desires of their own. Popular music and films also reflected this change in attitude. "What's Love Got to Do with It?" sang rock singer Tina Turner. Physical love is a natural act,

she sings, one that doesn't require emotional love. Madonna's 1986 hit song "Papa Don't Preach" is about a young girl who becomes pregnant. The film *For Keeps* (1988) also addressed teen pregnancy. Actress Molly Ringwald portrayed a high school honor student who gives up her dreams of a college education and a career as a journalist once she learns she is pregnant.

Sassy magazine was a newcomer to the teen magazine market in the 1980s. According to *Sassy* staff member Elizabeth Larsen, the magazine's mission was to educate girls about female sexuality, but not as a way to promote sexual promiscuity. Articles on methods of birth control or those with titles such as "The

Truth about Boys' Bodies" and "Getting Turned On" were, said Larsen, "written to let girls know that whatever choices they made about their sexuality weren't shameful as long as they were responsible about safe sex, birth control, and emotional self-care."

Sassy was among the first magazines to acknowledge that adolescent girls often struggled with sexual identity. Among the choices all men and women face is the choice of a sexual partner. Popular culture of the 1970s and 1980s popularized heterosexual relationships, or those between males and females. Missing from the media's message on sexuality were homosexual relationships, or those between same-sex partners. In the 1970s, articles on homosexual relationships were rare. Even so, same-sex relationships existed. More often than not, they were secret relationships. Homosexuals had been society's outcasts. In the 1960s, gay pride groups had formed to promote rights for homosexual men and women. Author Rita Mae Brown resigned from NOW to protest leader Betty Friedan's anti-gay stance. Brown led an informal group dubbed the Lavender Menace. It successfully criticized the Friedan-led Second Congress to Unite Women in May of 1970 to the point that the 1971 NOW meeting formally recognized lesbian rights as a feminist concern. The efforts of such groups, plus the increasing awareness of sexuality, gave many

Gay rights leader Rita Mae Brown is a poet, Emmy-nominated screenwriter, and novelist. She is shown here with her cat Mr. Sneaky Pie Brown with whom she has "co-authored" a successful mystery series featuring several feline characters.

gay men and women the courage to break their silence. A new phrase, "coming out of the closet," entered the media's vocabulary. *Coming out* meant "stating publicly one's homosexuality." By the century's end, the media's focus on female sexuality was no longer limited to what men preferred.

"If You Let Me Play…"

The little girl sits on a swing. She looks into the camera and says, "If you let me play sports, I will like myself more." The camera cuts to another girl in the playground. She, too, is about eight years old. "If you let me play, I will suffer less depression. I will be 60 percent less likely to get cancer."

This playground has many girls, it seems. Each girl makes her own statement: "If you let me play sports . . .

"I will have more self-confidence . . ."

"I will be more likely to leave a man who beats me . . ."

"I will be less likely to get pregnant before I want to"

"I will know what it means to be strong. . . ."

Not until the late 1990s did ads featuring female athletes become commonplace. Here soccer star Mia Hamm appears in a Nike ad that celebrates the strong, firmly toned, female athlete. The ad promotes a look that is totally different from the waiflike look of earlier decades.

The television screen fades to black and a *swoosh* symbol appears. This symbol is the corporate logo for Nike, a company that makes sports clothing—shoes, in particular. But the commercial doesn't show any sports shoes. It shows only those wide-eyed girls seeking permission to play sports.

The "If You Let Me Play . . ." commercial first aired in 1995. It was an attempt to sell shoes to girls and not just boys, said Liz Dolan, Nike's vice president of marketing at the time. But it was also "a call to action," she said, "for parents, educators, and citizens . . . to understand that girls' sports are important."

How important? In just thirty seconds, the Nike commercial made a cause-and-effect link between females participating in sports and improved self-esteem. Playing sports is good for a girl's health, and Nike provided statistics to prove it. Nike cited medical studies that showed that as little as four hours of exercise a week can reduce a woman's risk of developing breast cancer. Another study indicated that one-half of all girls who play sports have higher-than-average self-esteem and suffer less depression. That confidence in themselves can, in turn, give them the willpower to say no to drugs and to pressure to have sex. They are also more likely to end a physically or verbally abusive relationship.

Said Dolan, "We had the information staring us in the face, so we said, 'Why don't we just state the facts?' Our intention was to be provocative; we wanted adults to think. The big breakthrough came when our agency said, it would be really arresting if you had the girls themselves saying these things."

Thirty years earlier, in 1965, few sports manufacturers had paid any attention to girls. It wasn't because female athletes didn't exist. They did. They always have. But men's sports dominated the media. Women's achievements in sports didn't make headlines or even news blurbs on the sports pages of many newspapers. In 1975 *Ladies' Home Journal* published an article on women superstars. It included photographs and brief biographies of Debbie Lawler, holder of the world record for the indoor motorcycle jump, and Barbara O'Brien, quarterback of the Dallas Bluebonnets, an all-female football team. But such magazine articles were rare.

Why did the media and the manufacturers ignore women's sports? One problem was the playing field. It wasn't level. In the 1960s, communities funded Little League programs for boys but not necessarily for girls. In the 1960s, many high schools and colleges funded men's sports programs. They promoted their teams through community booster clubs, which raised additional money for uniforms and equipment. Funding for female sports program was usually much less. As a result, young women didn't have the equipment or the opportunities to develop their athletic skills.

Another study indicated that one-half of all girls who play sports have higher-than-average self-esteem and suffer less depression.

In 1972 Title IX leveled the playing field. This law was passed in part through the efforts of the women's liberation movement. The new law prohibited discrimination at schools, as well as in prisons, museums, and other public and private institutions. It meant that a school district had to fund sports programs for girls as well as for boys. If a school provided facilities and equipment for its male athletes, then it had to provide similar facilities and equipment for its female athletes. If a college provided scholarships for male athletes, it had to provide scholarships for female athletes too. Title IX also made sexual harassment illegal. The law was controversial. Many schools feared that the expense would end all sports programs, for males and females, if forced to provide equal opportunities for both.

In 1972 colleges spent 98 percent of their athletic budgets on men's sports. Women's sports programs received just 2 percent. With Title IX came increased spending on women's programs. The result was greater participation of girls in sports. Before Title IX, young women were 7 percent of the students participating in high school sports. By 2001, 2.8 million young women, or 41.5 percent, participated in high school sports.

Media attention on women's sports and female athletes also began to increase, although slowly. Not until 1987 did *Sports Illustrated* feature a female athlete on its cover. She was track star Jackie Joyner-Kersee.

With the growing popularity of women's sports, Nike saw an opportunity to sell its products to a new market of females. "If You Let Me Play" became one of the most talked about commercials of the 1990s. Nike was selling more than athletic shoes. It was selling women's self-esteem. Women's groups applauded the message that sports weren't just games but a women's health issue. Even so, it took Nike—and many Americans—a long time to figure it out.

Women Make News, 1976—the Yale Women's Protest

Sweaty, with sore muscles, the women's crew team waited thirty minutes on the bus. They had spent the last hour working hard on the Housatonic River in New Haven, Connecticut. Crew is a rowing sport. Each team member in a lightweight boat—called a scull—pulls hard, fast, and in unison. The sport has a rich history at Yale, long a male-only university. When Yale admitted women to classes in 1969, it also admitted them to the sport of rowing. After a hard workout on the river, members of the men's team headed to the Yale boathouse to shower. The boathouse was for men only. It had no showers or

A Hero for Daisy

Mary Mazzio competed in the 1992 Olympics as a member of the U.S. women's crew team. A few years later, she gave birth to a daughter, Daisy. The former Olympic athlete began to wonder whom her daughter's heroes might be. She didn't want Daisy to worry about whether she was as pretty or as slim as the magazine models or department store mannequins. She didn't want her daughter to view her body as a decoration. "I want her to be able to exert effort, and discover her limitations, and get out there, and get sweaty, and get dirty, and know she doesn't have to look gorgeous to have value in this society," said Mazzio.

In 1999 Mazzio made a documentary film about Chris Ernst and the Yale women's protest of 1976. She titled it *A Hero for Daisy*. She made the film not only for her daughter but for all future female athletes, hoping to inspire them to great accomplishments, both on and off the field.

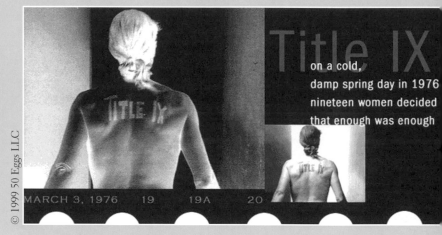

© 1999 50 Eggs LLC

The demonstration of the Yale women's crew team became the subject of a 1999 film, which the New York Times, Sports Illustrated, *and* TV Guide *praised for its inspirational message about and for women. The film, a clip from which is shown above, directed national attention to the financial inequalities and physical realities of women's athletics.*

even bathrooms for women. When the men's crew had finished cleaning up, and putting on dry clothes, the women still weren't allowed into the locker rooms. They rode home on the bus to their dormitories.

The women were angry as well as cold. Some got sick while sitting on the bus and waiting. They faced other discrimination as well. When they entered the gym to lift weights—an important part of crew training—the men laughed, jeered, hissed, and otherwise insulted them. "You have no idea how that felt, as an eighteen-year-old female to whom it was very important to be attractive and sexual somehow," said Anne Warner, a member of the team, "to have these large men somehow, your peers, judging you as somehow disgusting and debased because you were strong and excelling."

One cold winter day in 1976, the

women's crew team came up with a plan to fight back. Title IX had made discrimination against females in educational institutions illegal. The team planned a protest. To be sure their voices were heard, they invited a reporter for the *New York Times* to come along.

On March 3, the women—nineteen in all—walked into the office of the Yale women's athletic director. Leading the march was team captain and two-time Olympic athlete Chris Ernst. The women pulled off their sweatshirts. Each woman was bare chested. Printed in blue magic marker—some across the back and some across the chest—was *Title IX*. The stunned athletic director listened as Chris Ernst read a statement. "These are the bodies Yale [is] exploiting," the Olympic champion began. "On a day like today, the ice freezes on this skin, then we sit for a half hour as the ice melts and soaks through to meet the sweat that is soaking us from the inside."

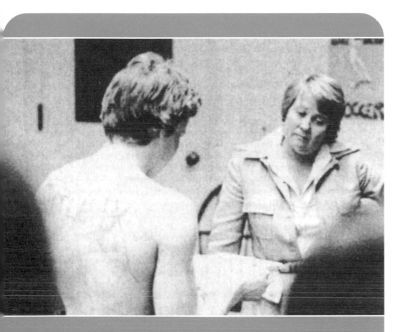

In 1976 Chris Ernst, Yale oarswoman and two-time Olympian, was caught by a photographer as she led a group of nineteen of her teammates into the office of the Yale women's athletic director. The women demonstrated against the lack of facilities for women rowers. Stripped to the waist, the protesters' backs and chests bore the phrase Title IX. The phrase refers to the federal law passed in 1972 that states that any program receiving government funding must provide equal opportunities to both genders.

The next day, the *New York Times* published the story about the protest with the headline, "Yale Women Strip to Protest Lack of Crew's Showers." Other newspapers picked up the story as well. Within hours, Yale began receiving telephone calls and letters supporting the women's demands for equal treatment and equal facilities. Two weeks later, the women's crew team had their showers. They had won something else as well: respect for female athletes.

Women Make News, 1997— WNBA Got Net

Lisa Leslie was born in 1972, the same year Title IX became law. It takes time to build an athletic program, train athletes, and put together a winning team. By the 1990s, a new generation of female athletes had grown up with the advantages of federally funded sports programs. They were coming on strong. On the tennis court, volleyball court, and basketball court—female athletes were lean, muscular, agile, and quick. As Olympic athletes representing the United States, they took home medals of all colors. *Time* magazine called the 1996 U.S. female Olympians "the girls of summer." The "girls" wanted more than just medals as amateur athletes. They wanted to play professional sports, just like the boys.

In 1996 the Board of Governors of the National Basketball Association (NBA) approved the formation of the Women's National Basketball Association (WNBA). Within months the league's eight teams had drafted players from among the best in colleges across the country. Lisa Leslie, who had won a gold medal along with her teammates in the 1996 Olympics, was one of the first women to sign with the WNBA. She would go on to become the league's highest scorer.

By then many American women who had graduated from college were playing basketball as paid professionals in Europe. Penny Toler returned to the United States to try out for the new WNBA. The first professional women's game, the New York Liberty against the Los Angeles Sparks, took

Penny Toler (center) *became a point guard for the Los Angeles Sparks in the 1997 WNBA draft. She is remembered as being the first player to score a basket in the WNBA. She did so against the New York Liberty in the June 21, 1997, game (above). Toler also made the first free throw in the league.*

A Mattel employee poses with a WNBA Barbie doll at the American International Toy Fair in New York. The doll debuted in February 1999 as part of a line of commemorative NBA Barbies.

game. But another slogan, printed on souvenir T-shirts, became popular during the WNBA's first season. The slogan was, "Invented by a Man, Perfected by a Woman."

As Lisa Leslie had hoped, the women's league drew flocks of young female fans to each game. To show their appreciation of the fans, the WNBA started a ritual called the ball exchange. The players come onto the court, each with a basketball. They then hand off the ball to a girl in the stands. Passing the ball to a younger woman in the stands suggests that the accomplishments of the women on the court will benefit future female athletes. After all, the person with the ball controls the game.

Nike, General Motors, Coca Cola, and Lee (jeans) are just some of the corporations that sponsor television commercials during the broadcasts of the women's games. In 1998 toy maker Mattel created a WNBA Barbie. Dressed in a league uniform, the doll came with her own doll-size basketball, warm-up jacket, towel, and water bottle. A photograph of a WNBA player appeared on the cover of the package. But there was still one problem: Barbie's shoulders, arms, and thighs were mannequin smooth. She lacked the fine-toned muscles of a real-life athlete.

place on June 21, 1997. At 19:01 on the clock, Sparks guard Penny Toler sunk the first basket and made women's sports history.

The WNBA's slogan is "We've Got Net." The phrase is commonly used at public playgrounds and basketball courts when a group of players reserves the court for the next

Chapter four

THE Material World, or Welcome to the 1980s

If you've got it, flaunt it!

Madonna fans at a Florida concert, 1985

HER HAIR *was* DIRTY BLONDE.

Then it was platinum, then red, then black, and then brunette. Sometimes it was streaks of multiple colors. She wore fishnet stockings and lace, but not always. She appeared onstage in a cone-shaped bra or a slinky evening gown with a fur stole. She was a rock singer, a dancer, an actress, and a video music star. A smart businesswoman, she created her own record company. She developed her own line of clothing, which sold well during her concert tours. Men didn't stand a chance with her unless they had cold cash, because she lived in a material world, and she was a material girl.

Madonna's appeal is partly her chameleon-like image. She is constantly reinventing herself, using fashion, music, and the media. She can be sweet, then sour, innocent, then raunchy. As her career took off, she was everywhere—on MTV, Broadway, television talk shows, and magazine covers. Her fans copied her images. Madonna wannabes wore ripped stockings and lace one year, then tube skirts and chains another. Her critics loathed her, usually for the same reasons her fans loved her—she was rebellious, independent, crass, and commercial. She didn't care what the magazine models wore. If a boy didn't give her "proper credit," she'd leave him, at least she said so in a song. Madonna was also incredibly successful. In 1985 she sold 16 million singles and albums. She was so popular that Macy's department store created "Madonnaland" to sell the style of clothing Madonna was currently wearing during her performances.

One of the most successful recording artists of all time, Madonna is also a dancer, songwriter, film producer, actor, author— and fashion icon. Shown here at the 1984 MTV Awards in New York City, she is wearing white lace lingerie, pearls, and a Boy Toy belt.

The *New York Times* summarized Madonna's celebrity in 1985. It stated, "Only those who have been residing on the planet Jupiter for the last several years need to ask Madonna who?" But while people knew about her, *who* she was remained a media riddle. Madonna displayed so many different personas that no one could say for certain just who the real woman was. Who she was *not* was easier. She was not a Stepford wife, a glam crime-fighting angel, or any of the popular media images of women from the 1970s. Was she a feminist? Some women said yes. Others argued that her lyrics as well as her clothing and behavior in some of her performances were demeaning to women. One thing everyone seemed to agree upon was this: Madonna was a cultural phenomenon of the 1980s.

"She's a product of the shopping-mall culture," journalist Dave Marsh said of Madonna. "But there's also a real rock side to her, a side that's independent and honest, that says, 'You don't like me, that's your problem.'"

having it all meant power, status, sexual freedom, and money.

The United States in the 1980s was "a culture of money and glitz," said journalist Peter Jennings. "Wealth and its excesses became a public fascination." "If you've got it, flaunt it," was a popular saying. Madonna's material world was one of designer labels and the belief that one person could have it all. Having it all meant power, status, sexual freedom, and money. "Millionaire?" wrote Peter Jennings about the United States' new wealthy class in the 1980s. "Try decamillionaire, centimillionaire, even billionaire." The decade boasted fifty-one billionaires, he reported.

As the 1980s began, conservative voters elected a former Hollywood movie star, Ronald Reagan, as president of the United States. Conservative voters also defeated the passage of the Equal Rights Amendment. Although many people predicted the end of the women's liberation movement, that didn't quite happen.

Don't Call Him Mr. Mom

Jack Butler has it all—a beautiful wife, great kids, a large home—until he loses his job. To maintain their lifestyle, Jack has to find a job in a hurry. He doesn't, but his wife, Caroline, does. *Mr. Mom* was a 1983 movie about parents who trade roles. He carries groceries and changes diapers. She carries a briefcase and writes advertising slogans.

The laughs begin when Dad learns just how challenging and confusing raising children can be. He heats up his son's grilled cheese sandwich using an iron. He dries the baby's bottom with a blow-dryer.

Although a comedy, the movie touched upon a real concern for married career women: how to succeed at work and still care for their families at home. News articles began to question if families were suffering because women were working. Do you remember moms? wrote reporter Alan Richman in the December 24, 1984, edition of the *Boston Globe*. They existed, he said, before the women's liberation movement, before both mommy and daddy became professional working parents.

The 1983 film Mr. Mom *was based on the life of Don Demers, an engineer who was laid off from his job and decided to raise his children while his wife worked as an emergency room nurse. Teri Garr and Michael Keaton play the husband-wife duo.*

Many working moms did not leave home to earn money for material items for themselves. Many worked to pay basic household bills, including those for doctors, cars, and clothing.

Mr. Mom hit a nerve with fathers too. Mr. Mom's incompetence might have been funny, but real-life, stay-at-home dads resented the stereotype that men could not be good parents. By the end of the 1990s, almost 200,000 men had opted to leave their jobs to become caregivers at home while their wives worked.

"*Mr. Mom* is like fingernails on a chalkboard to the stay-at-home fathers," said Bill Dow. In 1997 Dow gave up a sixteen-year career as a lawyer to care for his children while his wife returned to work. "The phrase 'Mr. Mom' is sexist," he said. "After all," he pointed out, "society does not call wage-earning women 'Mrs. Dad.'"

Women continued to challenge and change their roles in society. Like Madonna, women went everywhere—in corporate boardrooms, on the Supreme Court, even in space. Women, too, wanted it all. Their appointments, achievements, and lifestyles still created controversy. In the 1980s, many adopted the Madonna attitude: "If you don't like me, that's your problem."

The Material Girl in the White House

Although many Americans loved their new president, his wife was another story. According to CNN news files, many Americans thought Nancy Reagan was a snob. As a younger woman, Nancy Davis had been a Hollywood actress. She gave up her career in the 1950s to become the wife of Ronald Reagan and to raise their children, Ron and Patty. The negative publicity about Nancy Reagan began soon after the voters of California first elected Ronald Reagan governor in 1966. She refused to live in the governor's mansion because it was so shabby and in need of repairs. Instead, the governor and his wife rented a more elegant home in a fashionable neighborhood. That's when the snob label first appeared.

When Nancy Reagan became First Lady of the United States in 1980, she wasn't too happy with the condition of the White House, either. This time, however, she couldn't move somewhere else. Like it or not, the White House was home. The First Lady raised money from wealthy friends and political supporters to renovate the interior

Nancy Reagan is shown in 1981 in the White House. The former First Lady's views on feminism are best expressed in a quotation from her book I Love You, Ronnie: *"I think a woman gets more if she acts feminine."*

rooms. Over the century, other First Ladies, including Jacqueline Kennedy in the 1960s, had also made renovations. But somehow Nancy Reagan's choice of lemon yellow furniture with a pale yellow rug in the family quarter's living room and the salmon furnishings with peach carpets in the bedroom seemed extravagant. It might have been the color scheme. Or maybe it was the price tag of more than $800,000.

This humorous "Queen Nancy" postcard reflects the feelings of Americans who felt that Nancy Reagan was aloof and demanding. Others, however, admired her regal demeanor, her total devotion to her husband, and the care that she took with domestic matters.

Then there was the dinnerware. Soon after moving into the White House, the First Lady purchased new china. It might have been the number of plates, cups, saucers, and finger bowls—4,370 pieces (enough 19-piece place settings for 220 people)—that seemed excessive. Or again, it might have been the choice of style—bands of striking scarlet crosshatched and edged with gold. Scarlet red was Nancy Reagan's favorite color, the media reported. The White House defended the expenditure. There weren't enough matching dishes to accommodate all the guests at one time. And a foundation, not the U.S. taxpayers, had paid the $209,508 bill. Nancy Reagan insisted that her recent purchases were not a change of habit after her husband was president. "I am just being myself," she said.

Nancy Reagan was a forceful, independent woman and fiercely loyal to her husband. She did not shy away from the flashing cameras. But she did say once that she hoped the press would not "stereotype" her. That was exactly the intention of a photographer named Alfred Gescheidt. He doctored a photograph of the First Lady, superimposing a crown and robe. He titled it "Queen Nancy" and created a postcard. Copies of it began appearing in Washington, D.C., gift shops. The *New York Times* described the postcard: "The gold crown is studded with costly jewels. The dress is of finest brocade. The cape is snowy ermine. But the majestic woman on what may be Washington's best-selling postcard is not, on second glance, Queen Elizabeth II of Britain. It's Nancy Reagan." The image was a fake. But the sentiment suggested that a material girl had moved into the White House.

While campaigning for president in 1980, Ronald Reagan had made a few promises to voters. One was to cut government spending. The country was experiencing high inflation, in which prices increase, but most people's wages do not keep up. On the day he took the presidential oath of office, however, Ronald Reagan angered some Americans by wearing a formal morning suit (a type of tuxedo worn during the day rather than the evening) that cost $1,250. The

the New York Times published more than one letter from readers who felt the First Lady's designer clothing was insensitive to those American families who were having to make do with less.

previous president, Jimmy Carter, had worn a $175 business suit on his inauguration day in 1976. Nancy Reagan's wardrobe also came under attack. The *New York Times* published more than one letter from readers who felt the First Lady's designer clothing was insensitive to those American families who were having to make do with less. The First Lady, wrote one woman, had "the insensitive gall to wear a dress that costs as much as a sports car" when the letter writer's family was having hot dogs for dinner.

Ronald Reagan would be president for eight years, dominating the decade. And Nancy Reagan wasn't going back to California anytime soon. Nor was she about to change her style and spending habits.

Lady Justice

Another of Ronald Reagan's campaign promises in 1980 was to appoint a woman to serve on the Supreme Court of the United States. He did not break his promise. In 1981 he nominated Sandra Day O'Connor, an attorney from Arizona. She was much respected but little known beyond her home state. Many conservatives across the country disapproved of the president's nomination of O'Connor. They believed she would support controversial political decisions, such as a woman's right to an abortion and equal rights for women. "We feel betrayed," said one conservative who had worked toward getting Reagan elected. "Dismayed," is the word Dr. Carolyn Gerster used to describe her reaction to O'Connor's nomination. Gerster was a past president of the National Right to Life (an antiabortion group), and she vowed to oppose O'Connor's nomination. In the nominee's defense, an Arizona attorney stated that O'Connor was "as concerned about women as she is concerned about people generally, but she's certainly not a radical feminist."

The president nominates a candidate to the Supreme Court. The Senate must approve the appointment through hearings and then a vote. During the weeks prior to the hearing, the media scrambled to learn what they could about O'Connor. She had grown up on a ranch in Arizona. By the time she was nine, she could rope a calf, mend a fence, and drive a truck. She was a whiz at school. After college graduation, she went to Stanford Law School, where she graduated among the top students in her class. She met her husband at law school. They married and started a family.

Starting a career in law, however, proved difficult for O'Connor. She applied to law firms, but they turned her down because she was a woman. "I interviewed with law firms in Los Angeles and San Francisco," she told a reporter from *Time*, "but none had ever hired a woman before as a lawyer, and they were not prepared to do so." One firm, however, offered her a job as a legal secretary. Instead of taking what would clearly be an inferior job given her education, she decided

"*i interviewed with law firms in Los Angeles and San Francisco,*" *she told a reporter from* Time, "*but none had ever hired a woman before as a lawyer, and they were not prepared to do so.*"

—*Sandra Day O'Connor as quoted in "The Brethren's First Sister,"* Time, *July 20, 1981* to start her own law practice. Within years, she had become a judge, then a state senator. She had a reputation as fair but hard. A fellow senator who disagreed with her once snapped, "If you were a man, I'd punch you in the nose." O'Connor fired back, "If you were a man, you could." The message was clear—O'Connor was not going to be intimidated.

As the news articles appeared, an image of the future female justice began to emerge. She had the grit of an Arizona cowgirl, and no one was going to put her down or push her around. She made delicious Mexican food. She could tell a funny story. She danced gracefully.

On the day of her Senate hearing, Sandra Day O'Connor sat before the men who would decide if she would become the first woman ever to serve on the U.S. Supreme Court. Cameras flashed as she answered each question.

Did she support the death penalty? She did.

Did she support school busing to ensure integrated schools? Sometimes, she said, busing is not beneficial for children. As a child, she had ridden a bus 75 miles (120 km) a day, to and from school and her parents' ranch. She had not enjoyed the experience.

The most controversial issue of all was on a woman's right to abortion. Did she agree with the 1973 Supreme Court decision on *Roe v. Wade*, which supported a woman's right to an abortion? Her answer was neither yes nor no. She said, "For myself it is simply offensive. But, I'm over the hill. I'm not going to be pregnant again. It's easy for me to say now." The conservatives weren't happy, but they were never able to pressure the

In September 1981, Sandra Day O'Connor (above) was sworn in before the Senate Judiciary Committee at her U.S. Supreme Court confirmation hearing. Commenting on her historic appointment, she said that the important thing was not that she would decide cases as a woman but that she was a woman who would get to decide cases.

conservative Republicans in Congress to block the nomination.

Days later, Sandra Day O'Connor sat in another room while the Senate cast its vote on her appointment. She said it was the longest five minutes of her life.

The Supreme Court has nine justices. In 1981, the year Ronald Reagan became president, the Supreme Court had existed for 191 years. In that time, 101 judges had served on the Supreme Court. All were men. The media often referred to the Supreme Court as the brethren (brothers). All that was about to change as the vote came in 99–0 in favor of O'Connor. Her appointment elevated the status of women. For the first time in U.S. history, a woman judge would sit on the highest court of the land. The brethren were getting a sister.

The Flip Side of Flaunting It

Madonna's material world didn't materialize for everyone. In cities and towns across the country, many women struggled to make ends meet. If "having it all" meant power, status, and money, then "making ends meet" meant food, clothing, and a place to live.

While the upper class grew in the 1980s, the middle class shrank. Some middle-class families had prospered and climbed upward. Many more, however, slipped downward into poverty. As a result, the number of homeless people grew. Both men and women were homeless in the United States in the 1980s. But the number of women who could no longer make ends meet for themselves and their children grew significantly. No one knew for certain just how many homeless people roamed U.S. cities and towns. In 1981 New York City social workers estimated that as many as six thousand women were homeless in that city alone.

By 1986 the number of homeless people sheltered by New York City had climbed to twenty-seven thousand. One-half of these were children in families headed by single women. Images of homeless women and children did not appear in glossy magazines. Nor were they the subject of television situation comedies. They were more often the subject of newspaper articles. But a person didn't have to turn on the television set to see a homeless man, woman, or child. Often, especially in big cities, they only had to look out their windows. Homeless people slept over heat grates on sidewalks in winter or curled under newspapers or plastic garbage bags on park benches and doorsteps of churches. By day some sat on the curb begging spare change from those who passed by. They stood in lines at homeless shelters and

A homeless woman lies on a bed at a shelter in New York City. As the number of homeless women and children rapidly increased during the late 1980s and 1990s, conditions in shelters deteriorated because of overcrowding.

soup kitchens, hoping for a bed for the night or a hot meal.

Many factors contributed to this growth in poverty in the United States in the 1980s. One factor was the shift from more liberal government policies to conservative policies. U.S. conservative leaders reduced funding for many welfare programs, including low-income housing and community social services. Less low-income housing meant fewer people could afford a place to live.

Another factor was divorce and domestic violence. Some divorced women were unable to pay for housing on a single income. Others escaped from relationships where they had been beaten or mentally abused. Studies have shown that a majority of homeless women in the 1980s had been physically beaten prior to leaving their homes. These women left behind more than a house and possessions. They lost a husband's income and social contacts, including friends and relatives. Even if a homeless woman found a warm bed in a community shelter, it was only a temporary solution. Eventually, the homeless person had to find something permanent. Too often she could not and ended up back on the streets.

Some women found help in homeless shelters. In Boston a run-down, old building, the former Milner Hotel, served as a temporary shelter for women and children. The hotel was filthy, a reporter discovered. Dead cockroaches littered the floor. But for a nineteen-year-old mother and her two-year-old son, the single room given them in the Milner was better than living on the streets.

not sleep well or long. The homeless must be constantly aware of danger—being beaten, for instance, or sexually assaulted. If a homeless woman found a safe shelter, ate nourishing food, and got much-needed sleep, her confusion often cleared. She could think about more than just where her next meal might come from. She could make plans. But for many women, that simply didn't happen.

If a homeless woman found a safe shelter, ate nourishing food, and got much-needed sleep, her confusion often cleared.

Many shelters were clean and safe, yet opposition to them still existed because of the stereotypical attitudes about the residents. In 1985 homeowners in a Los Angeles neighborhood vowed to prevent the city from turning a closed elementary school into a shelter. City officials argued that the shelter was for women and children, not winos or derelicts. Just as the rich are sometimes labeled heartless and greedy, the poor are often unfairly labeled too. According to the stereotypes, homeless men are alcoholics and tramps. Homeless women are bag ladies or mentally ill. Some homeless women were mentally ill, but some others only appeared to be. A homeless person on the street does

Ann Marie Rousseau was a photojournalist. As a student in the 1970s, she had no idea what life might be like for a homeless woman. Then she taught an art class at a women's shelter in New York City. The cultural stereotypes didn't fit many of the homeless women she met. For one thing, many of the women were young, not old. Some were runaway teens. Every homeless woman had a story, she discovered, and it wasn't always the same. Some women were drug addicts. Some were mentally ill. Other women were divorced or abandoned by their husbands. Some had children with them in the shelters, but many just had photographs of their children. Those children were living with

Photographer Ann Marie Rousseau's description of her pictures was as moving as the photographs themselves. She titled this one "The Benediction" because the gesture of the mannequins is the same one the pope often assumes. She comments, "To me this picture has a lot to do with women both on the inside and the outside. The homeless woman on the outside carries all her worldly possessions and wears everything she owns. The more privileged women (mannequins) on the inside advertise cruise wear in the dead of winter, and are portrayed half naked, bald and equally alienated. They bestow a blessing on their sister a world apart, yet only inches away on the other side of the glass. Both are in full view on public display and are at the same time, to the larger world, invisible."

relatives or in foster homes. Some women had been evicted from apartments or had lost jobs. Some had lived on the streets for many years. Others were new arrivals to the city, hoping that somehow they could change their lives for the better there.

As the photographer befriended the women, she began to travel with them, tak-ing along her camera. A homeless woman's best defense is crowds and light, Rousseau learned. That is why so many lingered near train stations and even emergency rooms of hospitals. Although crowds gave some degree of safety to the homeless women, they were often invisible to those who walked by. When taking photographs,

Rousseau tried to capture more than just the women's faces, hands, and soiled clothing. She framed their environments—the sidewalk in front of Macy's department store, a wall in the subway, or inside an all-night diner. In a public restroom, a woman might wash her arms, neck, legs, and feet—but quickly before a security guard forced her outside again.

In 1981 Rousseau published her photographs in a book called *Shopping Bag Ladies: Homeless Women Speak about Their Lives*. The book was the inspiration for a 1985 made-for-television movie called *Stone Pillow*. The star was Lucille Ball, a brilliant comedian best known for her role as a flighty housewife in the 1950s television comedy series *I Love Lucy*. The promotion for the show promised, "Once she made you laugh. Tonight she'll touch your heart."

In *Stone Pillow*, the talented actress became Florabelle, a homeless woman befriended by an idealistic social worker. After the deaths of several of her friends, all homeless people, Florabelle agrees to let the social worker help her. Stone Pillow was the second-highest-rated TV movie of the 1985–1986 television season. Critics, however, thought the story was sappy and melodramatic. Even "the queen of television" (as Lucille Ball had once been called) could not make the invisible bag ladies real. In the living rooms of those families who had televisions, refrigerators, beds, and bathrooms, the problem of homeless women wasn't much more than a compelling—albeit sentimental—story starring a beloved actress.

Lucille Ball broke out of her I Love Lucy *comic mode to pay Florabelle, a fiercely independent aging New York bag lady, in the 1985 television movie* Stone Pillow.

Perhaps photographs and news articles were a more effective way of communicating the plight of homeless men and women to Americans. Even so, this complicated social problem wasn't going to go away anytime soon. In fact, by the end of the century, the situation had worsened.

The "O" Revolution

"We live in a society that doesn't pay attention to you unless you have money or fame," said Oprah Winfrey. "The responsibility of people who have money and fame and some kind of clout is to use that in a meaningful way."

Winfrey is one of those people who has money, fame, and clout and uses them in meaningful ways. In the early 1980s, Winfrey was a television news reporter and news program coanchor in Baltimore, Maryland. Her news director was unhappy with her physical appearance, citing among other things that her nose was too wide and her chin too big. He encouraged her to change. What Winfrey eventually changed was not the size of her nose but her job. She left Baltimore for Chicago, Illinois. "Everybody, with the exception of my best friend, told me it wouldn't work," Winfrey later told an interviewer. "They said I was black, female and overweight. They said Chicago is a racist city."

"Everybody, with the exception of my best friend, told me it wouldn't work. They said I was black, female and overweight. They said Chicago is a racist city."

—Oprah Winfrey, quoted in the New York Times, *November 8, 2006*

Christa McAuliffe Touches the Future

In the 1980s, NASA launched an innovative project called the Teacher in Space program in which a teacher would present two lessons to the nation's children directly from a space shuttle. High schools social studies teacher Christa McAuliffe of Concord, New Hampshire, was selected from a pool of eleven thousand applicants to be the teacher in space.

Christa McAuliffe's dream was to inspire students to reach for the stars. "If I can get some student interested in science," she told reporters, "if I can show members of the general public what's going on up there in the space program, then my job's been done."

On the morning of the launch, January 28, 1986, millions of children gathered in school auditoriums or in classrooms in front of television monitors.

As the crew prepared to climb into the spacecraft, a member of the NASA support team stepped forward to hand Christa an apple. It was a traditional symbol of affection for a favorite teacher. She laughed. "Save it for me," she said, "and I'll eat it when I get back."

Seventy-three seconds into the flight, *Challenger* exploded. Television cameras that were broadcasting the launch captured a Y-shaped plume of smoke spiraling across the sky as the *Challenger* disintegrated. Stunned Americans, including millions of children, watched in disbelief. All crew members had died.

As part of her astronaut training, teacher Christa McAuliffe received a preview of microgravity on a "zero gravity" aircraft nicknamed the "vomit comet" because of the nausea that is often induced. McAuliffe represented the Teacher in Space program aboard the Challenger, *which exploded during takeoff on January 28, 1986, claiming the lives of the crew members.*

A.M. Chicago was a morning talk show at the bottom in television-viewing ratings. The show targeted stay-at-home moms. Winfrey changed the type of stories from "mascara and cooking" (as one journalist had described the show's content) to more social and even controversial issues, such as child abuse. She planned programs around themes of interest to women, many intended to boost women's self-esteem. Topics included parenting, divorce, weight control, alcoholism, and literacy.

It wasn't just the change in subject matter that boosted the show's ratings. It was also Winfrey's conversational style. She didn't lecture her audience or intellectualize social problems, wrote the *Miami Herald*. She felt the issues, the *Herald* stated, as if she had experienced them. Audiences loved her. Ratings soared so dramatically that within a year, the television station changed the name of the program to *The Oprah Winfrey Show*. Three years later, this popular talk show host proved to be a shrewd businesswoman as well. She gained ownership of the show.

Coming from an impoverished childhood, Oprah Winfrey rose to be the highest-rated talk show host in television history. Add to that her achievements as an actress, book critic, magazine publisher, and philanthropist, it is no wonder she is considered one of the world's most influential women.

Oprah Winfrey revolutionized daytime television, because of the controversial subjects she discussed and because of who she was—an African American woman who struggled with her weight and had survived a difficult childhood. "I am never not aware of who I am, where I've come from. . . ." Winfrey told an interviewer. "I am a colored girl born in Mississippi in 1954 and all that that means: poverty, isolation, discrimination, deprivation, lack of information, low self-esteem."

In another interview, Winfrey described herself this way: "When you get me, you are not getting an image, you are not getting a figurehead. You're not getting a theme song. You're getting all of me. And I bring all my stuff with me. My history, my past."

Her career soared far beyond her television audience of millions of Americans (predominantly women). She acted in films, including *The Color Purple* (1985) She founded Harpo Productions so that she could produce films and television programs to explore issues of concern to her—most often stories about women. She began a book club on her talk show. Publishers clamored to have Oprah discuss and recommend their books. They knew that all those faithful viewers would purchase a copy, thereby making it a best seller.

Winfrey was a material girl. She became very, very wealthy. She admitted too that she loved nice things and spent money on herself. However, she was a material girl with a mission. Winfrey gave millions to charities. She even founded her own charity, Oprah's Angel Network. In its first year, the Angel Network raised more than $3.5 million to fund college scholarships for young people who could not otherwise afford to go to college. So great was her influence that *Time* magazine named her to its list of the "100 most important people of the 20th century."

CHAPTER FiVE

GUERRiLLA GiRLS

AND OTHER MiLiTANT FEMALES MARCH iNTO THE 1990s

A STEREOTYPE IS A BOX, usually too small, that a girl gets jammed into. An archetype is a pedestal, usually too high, that she gets lifted up onto. Some archetypes can be stereotypes, like a Mother Teresa or even a Bombshell. . . . Stereotype or archetype, it's rarely a girl's own choice. **It's a label someone else gives you to make you less or more than you really are.**

—*Guerrilla Girls*, Bitches, Bimbos, and Ballbreakers (2003)

NO ONE WAS PAYING ATTENTION.

The women paced up and down the sidewalk in front of the Metropolitan Museum of Art in New York City. They held placards stating that the museum was discriminating against women. Passersby ignored them, as did the people who entered the museum.

The exhibit the women were protesting on that June 1984 day was called "An International Survey of Painting and Sculpture." A press release from the museum had stated that the show would feature the work of the most significant contemporary artists in the world. It was quite a promise. However, of the 169 artists in the exhibit, all were white and less than 10 percent were women. Women were artists too. Were men better artists than women? The women on the picket line thought not. They believed the difference in representation was a case of gender discrimination.

Which artists get reviewed in the media often depends on which artists the galleries and museums show. And so the cycle goes: An artist who doesn't show doesn't get reviewed. Without a review, the art public won't know or value the work and so won't purchase it. Without sales, how can artists continue to work? They couldn't, at least not as artists. That was the protesters' argument, but no one was listening.

Although discouraged that the picket line in front of the museum had been

Donning gorilla masks not only garnered attention to the Guerrilla Girls' campaign to achieve recognition for female artists but also protected their personal identities. They were, after all, attacking the art world in which they wanted to be displayed.

ineffective, a few of the women protesters did not give up. Instead, they decided the time had come for a new strategy.

First, they identified their mission: to raise the public's consciousness about discrimination against women artists using simple facts. Next, they gathered their ammunition: statistics. They did research. They went to museums and art galleries and simply counted the number of works by male artists as compared to those by female artists. They went to the library and read all the articles the *New York Times* had written about artists. They counted the articles by gender too. They discovered that most successful artists, those who could earn a living by their work, were white males. Many museum and gallery administrators were also white males. Many of the art critics and publishers of art magazines were white males.

The researchers thumbed through their college art textbooks to see which women, if any, were represented. They discovered that discrimination against women wasn't a trend of the 1980s or 1990s. Art historians pretty much ignored talented women artists throughout history too.

ART HiSTORiANS PRETTY MUCH iGNORED TALENTED WOMEN ARTiSTS THROUGHOUT HiSTORY TOO.

Armed with statistics, the group's next step was developing both a weapon and a plan of attack. Walking a picket line hadn't been effective. They could hold a press conference, but the press might not come. They could hand out leaflets, but passersby could simply toss them aside.

No, this time the group had to come up with something more brazen. They decided to become the Guerrilla Girls (GG). Guerrillas are small groups of fighters with unconventional weapons who take on

Do women have to be naked to get into the Met. Museum?

Less than 5% of the artists in the Modern Art sections are women, but 85% of the nudes are female.

GUERRILLA GIRLS Box 1056 Cooper Sta. NY, NY 10276
CONSCIENCE OF THE ART WORLD

Guerrilla Girls used a variety of techniques to get their points across, among them a series of thought-provoking advertisements and posters. This is one that they entered in a Public Art Fund contest in 1989. It was rejected. They then rented advertising space in New York City buses and ran the ad themselves until the bus company canceled their lease saying that the image was too suggestive.

larger, stronger forces. Humor and "outrageous visuals" would be the Guerrilla Girls' weapons. For their military uniform, they wore blue jeans and sneakers or shorts and tights. Each also donned a life-size rubber gorilla mask.

CAN FEMINISTS BE FUNNY?

"It's not easy spending hours in a gorilla mask," said one of the Guerrilla Girls. "But more conventional women's clothing—bras, tight skirts, high heels—isn't exactly easy either. At least gorilla masks have a higher mission. They get us attention."105

Gorilla and *guerrilla* may sound the same, but they have very different meanings. A gorilla is the largest member of the ape family. A guerrilla is a military rebel, a type of underground soldier who fights for a political cause, often the overthrow of a government.

The Guerrilla Girls didn't want to overthrow the U.S. government, of course. But they did want to change some governmental and cultural attitudes that promoted discrimination.

Guerrilla warfare tactics include espionage (intelligence), ambush (surprise), and deception (trickery). The women called themselves Guerrilla Girls for that very reason. Because they were artists, they understood the power of visual images. They started with two different posters identifying museums that favored male artists. They signed the posters, "Guerrilla Girls—Conscience of the Art World." Suddenly, mysteriously, copies of these posters began appearing along the streets of SoHo, a neighborhood in downtown New York City that is home to many galleries. Many artists also live there. The Guerrilla Girls ambushed art galleries, secretly pasting posters across windows and doors. "These galleries show no more than 10% women artists or none at all," the posters read. They attended lectures and gallery openings, wearing their masks. The war had begun.

How the Guerrilla Girls came to wear the rubber gorilla masks was the result of a spelling error. One of the art activists wrote *gorilla* when she meant *guerrilla*, but the mistake gave the group its identity. Wearing a *gorilla* mask to represent a *guerrilla girl* was a visual pun. But why wear a mask at all? Some artists may have wanted to protect their identities so that they could continue to work in the art world without being fired from their jobs for protesting policies. But that's not the real reason, insisted the Guerrilla Girls. They wore the masks,

GUERRILLA GIRLS DEMAND A RETURN TO TRADITIONAL VALUES ON ABORTION.

Before the mid-19th century, abortion in the first few months of pregnancy was legal. Even the Catholic Church did not forbid it until 1869.*

*Carl. N. Flanders, Abortion, Library in a Book, 1991

A PUBLIC SERVICE MESSAGE FROM **GUERRILLA GIRLS** 532 LA GUARDIA PL #237, NY 10012

they said, in order to focus attention not on who they were but rather the issues of female equality. Besides, adds a GG who called herself Georgia O'Keeffe (in honor of an American artist who was overlooked at that time), "guerrilla" sounds so good with "girl."

The mask wasn't the only way the activists hid their identities, however. They adopted the names of dead women artists they felt history had not given due credit to. These artists included German printmaker and sculptor Kathe Kollwitz and Mexican painter Frida Kahlo. Some GGs took on the names of female writers, such as Zora Neale Hurston and Gertrude Stein. The choice of an alias, or an additional name, was another way the women could bring attention to those artists that history had underrated when they were alive.

black bat or a boomerang, they said. A veteran of the war called it "a black gash of shame" and an insult. Another called the sloping ground "a degrading ditch."

The designer, Lin, was an art student at Yale University. The Fine Arts Commission in charge of building the memorial had chosen her design from more than 1,400 submitted. A reporter from the *Washington Post* described the young architect during a public hearing. "As people lashed out at her design," he wrote, "Lin sat in the room neither smiling nor frowning—stoic, quiet, like a granite wall."

Lin explained her idea to inscribe the more than fifty-eight thousand names onto the wall. One hundred years from now, said Lin, no one will know who those people were. But they will wonder. She proposed listing the names chronologically by date of death rather than alphabetically by name. But names would be easier to find if presented in alphabetical order, her critics claimed. Making it easy wasn't her intention. She wanted people to search and to consider how long the conflict had lasted.

Lin's design was controversial, not only because the artist was young, female, and Asian American but also because of the nontraditional design. Art critics gave it derogatory labels, such as giant tombstone. But those who wanted to honor fallen war heroes disagreed. Veterans and their families came by the thousands to the dedication (above) on November 13, 1982.

Lin believed that sculpture should be touched. "If you create something unusual, people will want to take the next step," she said. And that was why the ground sloped, so that people could walk into the memorial. That was why the walls were reflective black granite, so that the living could see themselves mirrored against the names of the dead. She had hoped her memorial would bring tears. In crying, touching the granite, or making a pencil rubbing of a name from the wall, families could honor the dead and begin to heal.

The Fine Arts Commission built the memorial as Lin designed it. In a compromise, they agreed to add—some distance away—a more traditional sculpture of soldiers in combat. In 1982 the U.S. National Park Service officially dedicated the Vietnam Veterans Memorial. People came—and continued to come. The Wall became the most visited memorial in the country. A directory helps mourners find the names they are searching for. As Lin had hoped, visitors touch the cool granite, and they cry. Some leave mementos at the base—everything from combat boots and war medals to high school graduation pictures and teddy bears. The National Park Service stores the tons of loving mementos left behind by mourners each year.

"Some day the Viet Nam memorial may win the hearts and minds of the American people," *Time* magazine wrote in 1981 during the debate over Lin's design. The magazine was right.

A FEMINIST IN THE WHITE HOUSE

The U.S. public cast nervous eyes at Hillary Rodham Clinton, just as a decade earlier it had viewed Nancy Reagan with trepidation. Politically, Nancy Reagan and Hillary Clinton were very different women. One was a Republican and a conservative, the other a Democrat. Yet both women have proven to be independent and ambitious. Like Reagan, Clinton was loyal to her husband, and she had been a determined supporter during his roller-coaster campaign for the presidency of the United States. During the 1992 campaign, Bill Clinton had stated that a vote for him was also a vote for Hillary. Not everyone thought that idea was funny or even wise. The press began to wonder, was Bill Clinton running for president? Or was Hillary?

Hillary Rodham grew up in a suburb of Chicago, became president of her high school class, graduated from Yale Law School, and dreamed of becoming a lawyer in a big-city practice. She met Bill Clinton while at law school, but their ambitions differed—at least geographically. He returned to his home state of Arkansas where he taught at the University of Arkansas and began a law practice. Soon after, Hillary Rodham traveled to Arkansas to be with him. When they married, Rodham kept her last name and did not take his. When Arkansas voters elected Bill Clinton governor, the state's first lady kept Rodham as her last name.

Hillary Clinton (standing right) did not let her official duties interfere with her private social agenda during her twelve years as first lady of Arkansas. Child advocacy was particularly important to her, and she founded the Arkansas Advocates for Children and Families. She is shown here in a Arkansas kindergarten class in the 1980s.

Arkansas voters "resented a feminist living in the Governor's mansion," reported *Time*. Eventually, she added Clinton's name. As attorney Hillary Rodham Clinton, she earned more than her husband and made some profitable investments. Twice, the *National Law Journal* named her one of the top one hundred lawyers in the country.

Just as the media microscope had focused on Nancy Reagan in the 1980s, so did the 1990s' media dissect Hillary Clinton's behavior and comments. During the 1992 campaign, an interviewer questioned her decision to maintain her law practice while first lady of Arkansas. Clinton said, "I suppose I could have stayed home and baked cookies and had teas, but what I decided to do was fulfill my profession, which I entered before my husband was in public life."

That statement turned out to be a sound-bite firecracker. Within thirteen minutes, the statement had flashed across news wire services. CNN picked up the story. The media called the comment the "cookies and tea incident." Was Clinton saying that stay-at-home

> ## "i SUPPOSE i COULD HAVE STAYED HOME AND BAKED COOKiES AND HAD TEAS, **BUT WHAT i DECiDED TO DO WAS FULFiLL MY PROFESSiON**, WHiCH i ENTERED BEFORE MY HUSBAND WAS iN PUBLiC LiFE."
>
> —Hillary Rodham Clinton, March 16, 1992

mothers were not as important as women who had careers? interviewers asked. No, she insisted. That wasn't her meaning at all. Some people sent her letters of support. Others wrote scalding letters that stated she was "an insult to American motherhood."

The media spotlight got hotter as the campaign progressed. Hillary Clinton had taken a leave of absence from her law practice. She resigned from various corporate boards to devote herself to being Mrs. Bill Clinton. Still, many in the Republican Party accused her of being a radical feminist. They questioned her family values. Had she not put her career before the care of her daughter and husband? If she hadn't stayed home to bake cookies before, she surely wasn't going to start baking cookies in the White House, they warned. She was going to influence her husband's policies.

Time magazine published a statement from former Republican president Richard Nixon about the potential First Lady. "Hillary pounds the piano so hard that Bill can't be heard. You want a wife who's intelligent, but not too intelligent," Nixon said. He continued, "If the wife comes through as being too strong . . . it makes the husband look like a wimp."

Not every accusation was inaccurate. Clinton herself had admitted to the press that if she were First Lady, she wanted to be involved with her husband's work. She could negotiate treaties, she suggested. She could work on labor issues. She said she felt passionately, as did her husband, about improving health care in the United States. She was highly intelligent. She had sat on the boards of large corporations, including Wal-Mart. She had been a successful lawyer. She looked forward to entertaining international guests at the White House. But she had so much more to offer than being a hostess. "I never expected that the way I defined my role as first lady would generate so much controversy and confusion," she would later state.

During a campaign appearance in Columbus, Ohio, a reporter said, "You know, some people think of you as an inspiring

Hillary Rodham Clinton became First Lady of the United States in 1993. She continued to work on behalf of children's rights as well as other family-oriented issues throughout her husband's presidency.

female attorney mother, and other people think of you as the overbearing yuppie wife from hell. How would you describe yourself?" *New York Times* journalist Maureen Dowd reported that "a hint of annoyance glittered" in Clinton's eyes. She answered that she was a wife, a mother, and an activist. She later added, "I don't think feminism, as I understand the definition, implies the rejection of maternal values, nurturing children, caring about the men in your life. That is just nonsense to me."

Clinton came to understand that the criticism leveled at her wasn't necessarily leveled at her personally. She gave herself some advice: "Take criticism seriously, but not per-

sonally. If there is truth in the criticism, try to learn from it. Otherwise, let it roll right off you." This was, she admitted later, easier said than done.

Clinton called the intense public attention the media microscope. There was simply no avoiding it. Right or wrong, she had become a cultural and political lightning rod. "I represented a fundamental change in the way women functioned in our society," she later wrote in her autobiography, *Living History*. "I was being labeled and categorized because of my positions and mistakes, and also because I had been turned into a symbol for women of my generation. That's why everything I said or did—and even what I wore—became a hot button for debate."

Bill Clinton won the 1992 election and became the forty-second president of the United States. The "cookies and tea incident" wasn't the first media firecracker Hillary Clinton had lit, and once she was the First Lady, it would not be the last. Just as Ronald Reagan's presidency had dominated the 1980s, so too would the Clinton presidency, also lasting eight years, dominate the 1990s.

WOMEN MAKE NEWS, 1993—TONI MORRISON'S NOBEL PRIZE IN LITERATURE

On October 7, 1993, it was announced that Toni Morrison had won the Nobel Prize in Literature. She became the first African American female writer to receive literature's most respected international award. And she was only the eighth woman in ninety years to win it. Toni Morrison grew up in a racially segregated world. But she also grew up in the presence of strong-willed women. They didn't call themselves feminists, she said. "I was surrounded by black women who were very tough and very aggressive and who always assumed they had to work and rear children and manage homes. They had enormously high expectations of their daughters."

Morrison was sixty-two years old when she won the Nobel Prize and had been writing for almost thirty years. Her first novel, *The Bluest Eye*, was published in 1970. More books followed in the 1970s and 1980s, among them *Sula, Song of Solomon, Tar Baby, Beloved*, and *Jazz*. "I want my books to capture the vast imagination of black people," Morrison said. "Black people have a story and that story has to be heard."

Writer Toni Morrison is congratulated by King Carl XVI Gustaf of Sweden after she received the 1993 Nobel Prize in Literature during the award ceremony on December 10, 1993. In an earlier essay, she described her approach as follows: "My work requires me to think about how free I can be as an African-American woman writer in my genderized, sexualized, wholly racialized world."

Hillary Rodham Clinton, like Nancy Reagan before her, would be under the microscope for a long time.

MURPHY BROWN HAS A BABY

Time called Murphy Brown "the woman who has it all but ain't got nobody." Murphy wasn't a real person. She was a television character portrayed by actress Candice Bergen. Murphy Brown was an updated, 1990s version of Mary Richards. Like Mary, Murphy was a single career woman. She had a mane of beautiful hair and a closet full of stunning clothes. Like Mary, Murphy worked in a newsroom. Murphy, however, wasn't an associate producer/producer. She was the star news anchor of *FYI*, a TV newsmagazine. Despite her success—or because of it—Murphy Brown had flaws. She was opinionated. Her ambition and feminist attitudes put a strain on her working and personal relationships. Her marriage had ended in divorce, and she dated only occasionally. Her career was her life.

Murphy Brown was a huge hit, because Candice Bergen was a fine comedian and the show touched upon current political issues. Murphy was funny. Her wisecracks were as sarcastic as a Guerrilla Girl poster.

During the 1991–1992 season, forty-year-old Murphy discovers she's pregnant. As a successful television journalist, she can easily afford to have a child. She worries, however, that as a career woman (and one without a husband), she may not be a good mother. Murphy Brown is the type of character who read books as a child instead of playing with dolls.

Murphy Brown's situation was fairly realistic. Single women do become pregnant and face the same difficulty deciding what to do next: Marry the father and have the child? Have the child but not marry the father?

There was another alternative—end the pregnancy. Abortion had been a controversial issue throughout the twentieth century. Murphy Brown believed in pro-choice. She considered abortion but rejected it. Instead, she chose to have her baby and become a single mom. The 1991–1992 television season ended with Murphy singing to her newborn infant cradled in her arms.

Viewers didn't have to wait until the fall season to learn what happened next. That spring Murphy's decision to raise a child on her own unexpectedly became part of the 1992 presidential election campaign. On May 19, 1992, Vice President Dan Quayle made a campaign speech at San Francisco's Commonwealth Club of California. He said, "Right now the failure of our families is hurting America deeply. When families fall, society falls. The anarchy and lack of structure in our inner cities are testament to how quickly civilization falls apart when the family foundation cracks. Children need love and discipline. A welfare check is not a husband. The state is not a father." The divorce rate in America was high, and as a result children were growing up in single-parent families. Quayle longed for a return to more traditional family values, he said, where children were wanted and grew up in a home with both a father and a mother. No doubt, many of those in the room shared his concern. Then he added, "It doesn't help matters when prime-time TV has Murphy Brown—a character who supposedly epitomizes today's intelligent, highly paid, professional woman—mocking the importance of fathers by bearing a child alone and calling it just another 'lifestyle choice.'" It wasn't just Murphy Brown, either, said the vice president. All of Hollywood routinely "jeered" at morality.

The TV sitcom Murphy Brown, *which ran from 1988 to 1998, did not shy away from issues, particularly those confronting women.* Murphy *herself was a recovering alcoholic, and in the last year of the show, she battled breast cancer. But it was her decision to have a child out of wedlock* (above) *that set off a national controversy.*

Like Hillary Clinton's cookies and tea incident, Dan Quayle's Murphy Brown comment made headlines. Images of the fictional Murphy Brown cradling her fictional infant appeared in *USA Today* with the headline: "Quayle: Murphy Brown No Role Model." The *New York Times* also ran the photograph. ABC's *World News Tonight* reported the story. The vice president quickly clarified his statement. He meant to stress the importance of a father in a child's life. He had great respect for single mothers, he insisted. He called them heroes.

The damage, however, had been done. Some in the media ridiculed the vice president for thinking Murphy Brown was real when she wasn't. Feminists and liberals accused the vice president of suggesting that single mothers were unfit parents. For weeks during the presidential election, the line between *reel* politics and *real* politics disappeared.

Whether people supported the vice president's position or not, he had made a controversial issue about women and families (as well as a fictional female character) front-page news. The debate over that issue would continue long after the election.

WOMEN MAKE NEWS, 1991 AND 1993: THE WOMEN WHO SAID NO

Over the final three decades of the twentieth century, women's roles in society changed. By the mid 1980s, more than half the college students in the United States were women. More women were majoring in traditionally male fields such as chemistry and engineering. In 1970 women comprised 38 percent of the total labor force in the United States. By 1995 that figure had grown to 46 percent.

More women worked full-time and more held management positions than women in the 1970s had.

Change may solve one problem, but often it triggers another. As more women entered the workforce, sexual harassment against those women increased. One reason was resentment. Women were entering what had previously been male-dominated workplaces, and incidences of harassment were higher in these jobs. Some men intentionally tried to make the women who had entered their domain uncomfortable. They did so by telling dirty jokes or making sexual comments about women's bodies or clothing. Many men believed that a woman's clothing and behavior—wearing short skirts or cursing, for example—were signals that she was "asking for it." "It" was sex.

In 1982 psychologist Joyce Brothers wrote a book titled *What Every Woman Should Know About Men*. Among the topics she addressed in the book was sexual harassment. "If it makes you feel uncomfortable, you are not misinterpreting it," she wrote. "It is sexual harassment."

BY THE MiD-1980S, **MORE THAN HALF THE COLLEGE STUDENTS iN THE UNiTED STATES WERE WOMEN.**

Yet no one—including the courts—could agree on just what sexual harassment was. Was it physical contact only, such as forced touching, kissing, or fondling? Or was it also verbal assaults, such as lewd comments, vulgar jokes, or name-calling? Did it exist only in the workplace between an employer and an employee? Or could it also happen in schools and colleges, the military, and public places, such as restaurants and theaters? Was harassment between a man and woman only, or could a person harass someone of the same sex? Could a woman sexually harass a man?

Sexual harassment was a complicated and frightening issue that affected a large number of women in the 1980s and 1990s. The courage of those women who stepped forward to file complaints, however, would bring the issue into public debate. They would help to clarify just what sexual harassment was and how to fight it.

For Anita Hill, a University of Oklahoma law professor, the harassment happened in the 1980s. Not until 1991, however, did she speak about it. She did so in the most public of places and times—in Washington, D.C., during televised Senate hearings on the nomination of Judge Clarence Thomas to the Supreme Court. If the Senate confirmed the nomination, Judge Thomas would become the second African American Supreme Court justice in U.S. history. (Thurgood Marshall became the first in 1967.) Thomas's nomination was controversial, in part because he was a conservative. Many civil rights supporters feared he might reverse civil rights legislation passed during the previous three decades. His nomination became more controversial after Anita Hill spoke under oath during the Senate hearings.

On October 11, 1991, Anita Hill (above) testifies to sexual harassment from former boss Clarence Thomas during a Senate Judiciary Committee hearing on the nomination of Thomas to the Supreme Court. Thomas would later win the nomination after a historic 52 to 48 Senate vote.

DO JOKES **HAVE A GENDER?**

A boy drinks eight colas and burps seven up. Funny? Or not funny?

A lifeguard at a public swimming pool shouts at a little boy, "Don't pee in the pool." The boys says, "But everybody does it." The lifeguard answers, "Not from the diving board." Funny? Or not funny?

Whether you laughed or did not laugh at those jokes may depend, in part, on your gender. "Men and women tend to have different opinions of what's funny," says feminist historian and author Regina Barreca. "Even when we happen to laugh at the same time we are not all laughing at the same things."

Burping and other natural body functions are often the stuff of male humor, especially in elementary and junior high school.

What is a sense of humor, however? For men it might be a woman who can take a joke. For women it might be someone who can tell a joke. There is a difference. Studies published in the 1970s by psychologist Paul McGhee indicated that society, in general, expected boys to be the teller of jokes. Girls were expected to be the listeners who laughed. Girls who told jokes were acting like boys.

Even so, in the last quarter of the twentieth century, more females found career success as comedians. Their humor was sometimes self-deprecating. In other words, the women made fun of themselves. They told jokes about being fat and ugly and lazy. Phyllis Diller made fun of her body as a way to get laughs. Roseanne Barr, a popular comedian of the 1990s who had her own weekly television program, often ridiculed her ability at (and lack of interest in) housework.

Women's humor was changing, just as their roles in society were changing. This joke about the handsome prince is an example:

Two women were walking down a New York street when they spotted a frog. The frog looked up and said, "I used to be a handsome, wealthy stockbroker. But I was turned into a frog. If one of you kisses me on the lips, I will be turned back to my original self." One of the women stooped down, picked up the frog and placed him in her pocket. The two friends walked on for a while, but the other finally got curious and said, "Aren't you going to kiss the frog on the lips and turn him back to what he was?" "Nope," she replied, "don't you know how much I can get for a talking frog these days?"

"It is only after a great deal of agonizing consideration and sleepless nights—a great number of sleepless nights that I am able to talk of these unpleasant matters to anyone but my close friends," she said to the Senate. Hill had worked as an assistant to Judge Thomas in the 1980s. After three months, he asked her out on a date. She refused, saying she thought it was ill-advised to begin a social relationship with her supervisor. Soon after, she charged, he began speaking with her, either in the privacy of his office or hers, about pornographic movies and sexual acts. He continued to pressure her into dating him and spoke about women's and men's body parts. The stress she suffered, she said, resulted in her hospitalization. Because of it, she eventually resigned and took a position elsewhere.

Why had she not come forward before? the Senate investigators, the media, and the many Americans who were watching the hearings on television wanted to know. "I was aware," she said, "that telling at any point . . . could adversely affect my future career."

The Senate hearings were not a court of law. The senators' task was not to determine if Anita Hill's accusation were true or false. Rather, the goal of the hearings was to determine if Clarence Thomas was qualified to serve as a Supreme Court justice. The Senate confirmed his appointment—but by a narrow margin of 52–48.

About the same time, navy lieutenant Paula Coughlin "blew the whistle" (as the media called it) on another sexual harassment incident. This one had occurred in Nevada in September 1991. The Tailhook Association, an organization of navy aviators, had held its annual convention at the Las Vegas Hilton hotel.

"i WAS AWARE **THAT TELLiNG (ABOUT JUDGE THOMAS'S ADVANCES) . . . COULD ADVERSELY AFFECT MY FUTURE CAREER"** —Anita Hill, 1992

WOMEN iN COMBAT

In 1970 women represented just 1.4 percent of military personnel. By the 1990s, that number had steadily increased to 13 percent. In 1996 thirty-two thousand women were in military uniform. Yet debate continued over what role they could or should play. Many in society still believed the stereotype that women were weak and emotional but men were strong and logical. Should women be allowed to fight on the front lines of battle? Could they pilot an attack helicopter? Many in the military thought the answers to those questions were no. Furthermore, integrating women into all-male combat forces would "undermine unit cohesion," some military officials stated. Women argued that until they could have combat jobs, they would "always suffer a second-class status that invites harassment."

In 1991 Congress repealed laws that barred women from combat and left the decision up to the individual military branches. By the end of the century, women in the military were serving in positions that had been predominantly male, including combat aviation and on naval combat ships.

In 1996 Carol Muller was the first-ever woman to achieve a three-star general status. Throughout her long military career, she saw many doors of opportunity open for women soldiers. Her three-star rank was just another door, she said.

In 1994 First Lieutenant Jean Flynn made history when she became the first woman to break into the once-exclusive male domain of U.S. Air Force combat pilots. She is shown here in 1998 as she climbs aboard an F-15E during her six months of tactical training in the 555th Fighter Squadron.

During the three-day convention, eighty-three women, some of them officers, and seven men were assaulted by their fellow aviators. Many of the male and female soldiers who attended the convention had served in the recent Persian Gulf War (1991) in Kuwait and Iraq. That war had ended, and the United States viewed its returning soldiers as heroes. But the navy aviators' behavior in the Hilton hotel seemed far from heroic. Women screamed for help as drunken aviators tore away their clothing and assaulted them. These were naval women, fellow soldiers, but the men seemed determined to humiliate them. Some of the aviators wore T-shirts they had printed for the convention that read, "Women Are Property." Not all naval aviators at the convention participated in the assault. Many who witnessed it, however, did nothing to stop it. Later reports indicated that some of the women attacked had been drinking. One naval officer told author Susan Faludi that some of the women had worn "sexy clothes" and were "dancing like a bunch of party girls."

The attack on Lieutenant Coughlin happened on Saturday night. While walking down the hallway of the third floor of the hotel, drunken Tailhook aviators grabbed her, shoved her, and tried to remove her clothing. She bit and kicked her attackers and eventu-

ally escaped. The next day, she reported the incident to her superior officer. According to a news reporter, he said, "That's what you get when you go to a hotel party with a bunch of drunk aviators." He warned her that filing a sexual harassment complaint about the Tailhook incident would seriously jeopardize her career in the U.S. Navy. She filed the complaint anyway, but the officer did not immediately forward the complaint to his superior officers. No other women stepped

Navy Lieutenant Paula Coughlin, the helicopter pilot and admiral's aid whose allegations of sexual assault at an aviator's convention in Las Vegas prompted examination of the U.S. Navy's attitude toward women, pauses outside a Las Vegas federal courthouse in October 1994.

forward. Coughlin was an officer. She believed the navy's code of ethics for conduct becoming an officer included speaking out when she saw or was the victim of an injustice. She told her story to the *Washington Post*. Soon other women who had also been assaulted during the convention stepped forward to agree with the lieutenant's story.

NOT ALL NAVAL AViATORS AT THE CONVENTiON PARTiCiPATED iN THE ASSAULT. MANY WHO WiTNESSED iT, HOWEVER, DiD NOTHiNG TO STOP iT.

Once again, sexual harassment became front-page news. Other stories of sexual harassment, not just in the military but also in military academies, surfaced. The military investigation into the Tailhook incident eventually resulted in 119 navy and 21 Marine Corps officers being cited for indecent assault, indecent exposure, conduct unbecoming an officer, and/or failure to act in a proper leadership capacity. None of these 140 cases ever went to trial. Approximately half were dropped for lack of evidence. The others ended with fines or severe career penalties. As for Lieutenant Coughlin, she eventually resigned her commission from the navy, citing continued abuse from fellow military personnel as a result of her sexual harassment charges.

Her superior officer was right. Filing the complaint had indeed ruined her military career. It had also damaged the careers of many other naval aviators, including some high-ranking officers. But it had served justice.

The Anita Hill testimony and the Tailhook scandal raised the media's—and men's and women's—awareness of the issue. A year later, a unanimous Supreme Court decision greatly clarified what sexual harassment was. The case was number 92-1168: *Harris v. Forklift Systems, Inc.*

From 1985 to 1987, Teresa Harris had worked as a manager for Forklift Systems, Inc., a truck leasing company in Tennessee. For two years, the company's president had made her feel uncomfortable. Very uncomfortable. According to court documents, he insulted Teresa Harris in front of her coworkers. He called her "a dumb ass." "You're a woman, what do you know?" he said. He suggested, again in front of other employees, that they go to the Holiday Inn hotel to negotiate Teresa Harris's raise, implying she was to give him sex. He made comments about her clothing. He also asked women employees to retrieve coins from his pants' pocket.

"At first I wanted to deny it was happening," Harris said. "Then I decided I would have to accept it and put up with it. I had two sons. I needed my job." Finally, in August 1987, she confronted her harasser. He was surprised that she had been offended. He claimed he had only been joking. He promised to stop. But he didn't. So at the age of forty-one, Harris decided she could no longer tolerate the workplace hostility. "I felt so hopeless," she said.

Teresa Harris (left) and her family share the news of the U.S. Supreme Court's 1993 groundbreaking decision in her favor in the sexual harassment suit against her former employer Forklift Systems, Inc.

In October 1987, she quit and sued her employer. She lost her case. The court agreed that the company president's behavior had been offensive but that it had not been "so severe so as to be expected to seriously affect [Harris's] psychological well-being."

Harris could have given up. Many people would never have dared to sue in the first place. But she didn't give up. Her lawyer appealed, and the case went to the Supreme Court. All nine U.S. Supreme Court justices agreed that Teresa Harris had been wronged. She had been sexually harassed, and under Title VII of the Civil Rights Act of 1964, no person shall be discriminated against because of race, religion, or gender. Furthermore, a woman didn't need to have a nervous breakdown to prove sexual harassment, wrote Justice Sandra Day O'Connor.

The Anita Hill Senate testimony, the Tailhook scandal, and Supreme Court case 92-1168 gave other women the courage to step forward and say no. The number of sexual harassment court cases increased dramatically in the 1990s. As awareness of the problem grew, so did efforts to combat it. The government, as well as businesses and schools, developed sexual harassment policies. They conducted training programs so that both men and women would understand what sexual harassment was: any unwanted or unwelcome behavior of a sexual nature, either physical or verbal, especially occurring in a context where one person has power over another.

"Not in our Navy" appeared on billboards on navy bases across the country following the Tailhook incident. But that doesn't mean that all military men would regard female soldiers and officers as their equals. Controlling a person's behavior through policy or laws is not the same thing as changing a person's attitude. Sexual harassment had not been on the law books as a form of discrimination in 1970. It was in the 1990s. Yet, despite the law, problems still existed because attitudes are hard to change.

*t*he girl power evolution

Brandi Chastain, Women's World Cup, July 10, 1999

*t*here are bigger things happening here
than just us winning a game. If we lose sight of that,
everything we did would be for nothing.

—Mia Hamm, 1999

"Well, the revolution is here,

and it has bright-red toenails. And it shops. And it carries diaper bags," reported *Sports Illustrated* in July 1999. The revolution wasn't about art, literature, politics, or war. The revolution was about women's sports. "The U.S. women's soccer team is towing the country around by the heart in this Women's World Cup, and just look at the players. They've got ponytails! They've got kids! They've got (gulp) curves!"

They also could perform well on the soccer field. Days before the *Sports Illustrated* article appeared, ninety thousand fans (including President Clinton) had filled the Rose Bowl in Southern California to watch the Women's World Cup finals. Fans spent millions of dollars on tickets to the event and women's soccer merchandise. Revenues totaled $23 million, proving that women's sports could be profitable. After a scoreless ninety minutes, the game went into two overtimes. American Brandi Chastain made the winning kick. The U.S. women's soccer team had defeated China. In a moment of pure joy, Chastain ripped off her uniform shirt and fell to her knees on the turf.

More than two thousand people from the media attended. The photograph of victorious Chastain, kneeling on the turf in her black sports bra, appeared across the country. The team made the rounds of television talk shows. Each time their plane landed in a new city, they were met by crowds of young girls eager to see them and get autographs. Suddenly, girl power was a good thing — strong, confident and, as *Sports Illustrated* pointed out, feminine too.

Who were these women? Some were single, some were married, and some were moms. They were all either college graduates or college students. They were tall, muscular, and fast. They worked out. They sang and danced to rock music and painted their toenails before games. And then, on the field, they were superb. They were feminists, and they were feminine. They were material girls who wanted to have fun, but they were guerrilla girls too. These women had grown up under the Title IX umbrella that had made discrimination based on race, religion, or gender illegal.

Revolution? No, said Marla Messing, president and chief executive officer of the Women's World Cup. It was *evolutionary*. The women's achievement had come as a result of decades of accomplishments.

Susan Amerson graduated in 1963 from a public high school that did not have a girls' athletic program. She always felt she had missed something. "I and other women have missed something by not being involved in real athletic competition on teams," she wrote to *Newsweek* following the World Cup finals. "I cannot imagine how qualities like determination, cooperation and joy could be termed 'unladylike.'"

Margaret Carlson, sportswriter for *Time*, had had a similar experience. She had played field hockey, she said, "with a stick that had duct tape around its base." Her coach was a nun from her school who relied on an instructional manual and prayers for a victory. "We sewed numbers on old gym suits to make them look like uniforms, while the guys wore miracle-fabric jerseys over molded plastic sufficient to protect them in the event of a nuclear attack," she wrote.

Fair? No, but that was before the Women's Strike for Equality. That was before Title IX. In 1970 the media portrayed women tossing away their bras. At that time, sports bras, like the one Brandi Chastain wore, didn't exist. "World Cup Fever seemed to signal that 27 years after Title IX legislation mandated equal financing for girls' athletics, women's team sports have truly arrived," *Newsweek* reported.

"i saw something in those girls' eyes—drive, pride, no thoughts of insecurity and a future that may never know glass ceilings."

—A women's soccer fan, quoted in *Newsweek*, August 9, 1999

And the fans agreed. Said one mother about the thousands of cheering girls in the Rose Bowl, "I saw something in those girls' eyes—drive, pride, no thoughts of insecurity and a future that may never know glass ceilings."

Stereotypes sink deep roots into society. As people challenge the old beliefs and create new opportunities, however, society changes. "Watch out," wrote one male fan. "These women are breaking records and knocking down the boundaries of sex and race. They won't be held back."

Series Afterword

Writing a book is a lot like taking a journey. We start out knowing where we want to go, but we don't know for certain just what we'll see and who we'll meet along the way. While writing this series on women's images and issues in the twentieth century, I met some fascinating women who have shown me things I did not previously know.

I began as the nineteenth century ended, in Chicago at the Columbian Exposition and continued through the turn of the century to the First World War (1914–1917). Here I met the feisty and independent Gibson girls and the suffragists. The Gibson girls drove motor cars and donned bloomers to play a new game called basketball. Some were ladies of polite Society, while others were immigrants who did their best to be fashionable on their paltry earnings. The suffragists, on the other hand, were more concerned with social justice than fashion and flirtation. They fought for the right to vote for all American women, demanded safer work conditions and better wages for working women, and called for better living conditions for impoverished families.

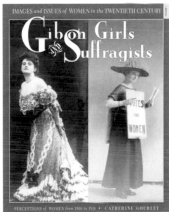

The second stop on my journey was the United States in the 1920s, where I was introduced to the flappers and the new American woman. How different the flappers were from any women who had gone before them, shocking society by dancing the Charleston, with bared knees, bobbed hair, and without a corset! The females the media called "new American women" were scientific mothers, using the latest scientific inventions to clean their houses and cook their families' meals. They were careful consumers, concerned with purchasing power and truth-in-advertising. Still others from this decade were college graduates, strong women who fought for equal opportunities alongside men in the workplace.

The stock market crash of 1929 began that period of American history known as the Great Depression. While traveling through these decades—the 1930s and 1940s—I met Mrs. America and Rosie. Mrs. America was a domestic paragon, learning how to make do with less. The media encouraged her to be the perfect mother—but not at the expense of her youthfulness or beauty. When men left for battlefronts, World War II (1939–1945) propelled many women to take their places in offices and factories. This movement spawned the hardworking, multitalented Rosie the Riveter.

The journey continued after the war, but the landscape was changing. Developers built suburban neighborhoods with tidy front lawns and backyard patios. Rosie gave up her job (often pressured by the government and the media to do so). In the 1950s, the young, blonde Gidget image offered young girls a role model for carefree living before they settled down to become wives and mothers. Yet many of the women of the 1950s and 1960s weren't buying the media images that advised them on how to catch husbands and bring up babies. Instead, they pursued the Woman Warrior persona to emerge as astronauts, activists, and challengers of bigotry and racism.

The final stop on the journey took me to the final three decades of the twentieth

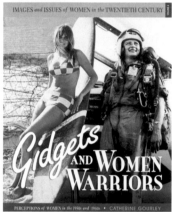

century, where I got to know Ms. and the Material Girls. The term *Ms.* was adopted by feminists—women who believe in equal pay for equal work, freedom from sexual harassment, and equal employment opportunities. The Material Girls wanted all this and more. They wanted to be wild, sexy, and outrageously fashionable—a modern version of their flapper sisters of decades earlier. And they also wanted control over their own lives—the kind of control that could only be achieved through money and legal rights to equal opportunities.

My journey covered a century. I was able to see a pattern, realizing that the women I met were all forging paths for their sisters to follow. Together they paved the way for the status that women enjoy in the twenty-first century.

I hope my readers have enjoyed the journey as much as I have.

—*Catherine Gourley*

4–5 Joan Jacobs Brumberg, *The Body Project* (New York: Vintage Books, 1998), xxxii.

6 Shirley Chisholm, "Equal Rights for Women," speech, House of Representatives, May 21, 1969, available online at *Special Collections Library, Duke University*, n.d., http://scriptorium.lib.duke.edu/wlm/equal/† (February 12, 2007).

8 Sara M. Evans, *Tidal Wave: How Women Changed America at Century's End* (New York: Free Press, 2003), 70.

9 Nicholas Johnson, *Test Pattern for Living* (New York: Bantam Books, 1972), 48.

10 *Time*, "Women on the March," September 7, 1970, n.d., http://www.time.com/time/magazine/article/0,9171,902696,00.html (November 9, 2006).

11 *Time*, "Who's Come a Long Way, Baby?" August 31, 1970, n.d., http://www.time.com/time/magazine/article/0,9171,876783,00.html (November 9, 2006).

12 Patricia Bradley, *Mass Media and the Shaping of American Feminism*, 1963–1975 (Jackson: University Press of Mississippi, 2003), 117.

12 Ibid.

13 Ibid., 118.

14 Letty Cottin, "The Working Woman," *Ladies' Home Journal*, March 1975, 66.

15 "Chisholm '72: Unbought & Unbossed," P.O.V., Public Broadcasting Station, n.d. http://www.pbs.org/pov/pov2005/chisholm/about.html (June 16, 2007).

15 John F. Kennedy Library, "A Tribute to Barbara Jordan and Shirley Chisholm," *John F. Kennedy Library Website*, n.d., http://www.jfklibrary.org/NR/rdonlyres/50647B18-6444-4306-B041-71AD30B32381/27391/MicrosoftWordATributetoShirleyChisholmandBarbaraJo.pdf (November 9, 2006).

15–16 *Time*, "Ms. President," February 7, 1972, n.d. http://www.time.com/time/magazine/article/0,9171,905714,00.html (November 9, 2006).

16 *Time*, "Madam President," March 20, 1972, n.d. http://www.time.com/time/magazine/article/0,9171,942515,00.html (June 16, 2007).

17 *Nation*, "Shirley Chisholm's Legacy."

17 Gloria Steinem, "President Chisholm," *Ms.*, January 1973, available online at *Point of View*, n.d., http://www.pbs.org/pov/pov2005/chisholm/special_ticket.html (November 9, 2006).

17 Linda K. Kerber and Jane Sherron De Hart, eds., *Women's America: Refocusing the Past*, 4th ed. (New York: Oxford University Press, 1995), 479.

17 Ibid.

21 Congress, House, Committee on Education and Labor, *Discrimination Against Women*, testimony of Pauli Murray, 91st Congress, 2nd Session (Washington, DC: U.S. Government Printing Office, 1970), available online at *History Matters*, n.d., http://historymatters.gmu.edu/d/6472 (February 7, 2007).

21 *Time*, "Martha Griffiths: Graceful Feminist," August, 24,

1970, n.d., http://www.time.com/time/magazine/article/0,9171,902638,00.html (November 15, 2006).

21–22 *Time*, "New Victory in an Old Crusade," August 24, 1970, n.d., http://www.time.com/time/magazine/article/0,9171,902637,00.html (November 9, 2006).

22 Linda Scott, *Fresh Lipstick: Redressing Fashion and Feminism* (New York: Palgrave Macmillan, 1994), 287–288.

23 *Time*, "For the Liberated Female," December 20, 1971, n.d., http://www.time.com/time/magazine/article/0,9171,878985,00.html (February 7, 2007).

25 *Time*, "Ms. Makes It," December 25, 1972, n.d., http://www.time.com/time/magazine/article/0,9171906720,00.html (November 9, 2006).

25 Susan Douglas, *Where the Girls Are: Growing Up Female with the Mass Media* (New York: Random House, 1994), 230.

26 The full-page advertisement for Hour After Hour deodorant can be found at Culture Cat, Rhetoric and Feminism, n.d., http://www.culturecat.net/node/983 (June 20, 2007).

29 *Time*, "Where She Is and Where She's Going," March 20, 1972, n.d., http://www.time.com/time/magazine/article/0,9171,942510,00.html (November 9, 2006).

29 Kerber and De Hart, *Women's America*, 536–537.

31 Ibid.

31 *Time*, "Anti-ERA Evangelist Wins Again," July 3,1978, n.d., http://www.time.com/time/magazine/article/0,9171,945990,00.html (November 9, 2006).

31 Phyllis Schlafly, "Beating the Bra Burners," *George*, June 1977, March 20, 2007, http://www.eagleforum.org/george/george.html (March 20, 2007).

32 *Time*, "Trouble for ERA," February 19, 1973, n.d., http://www.time.com/time/magazine/article/0,9171,906864,00.html (November 9, 2006).

32 Evans, *Tidal Wave*, 171.

33 *Time*, "Just One of the Guys and Quite a Bit More," July 23, 1984, n.d., http://www.time.com/time/magazine/article/0,9171,952426,00.html (November 9, 2006).

34 John T. Molloy, *Dress for Success* (New York: Peter H. Wyden, 1975), 1–3.

34 Ibid., 178–179.

35 Emily Cho, *Looking, Working, Living Terrific 24 Hours a Day: Get Your Life in Order with Personal Style* (New York: G. P. Putnam's Sons, 1982), 41.

36 Geraldine Ferraro, "Vice Presidential Nomination Acceptance Address," *American Rhetoric*, n.d., http://www.americanrhetoric.com/speeches/gferraroacceptanceaddress.html (February 7, 2007).

36 Cho, *Looking, Working*, 41.

36 *Time*, "A Credible Candidacy and Then Some," November 19, 1984, n.d., http://www.time.com/time/magazine/article/0,9171,950197,00.html (November 9, 2006).

36–37 Ferraro, "Vice Presidential Nomination Acceptance Address."

37 Maureen Dowd, "Taking the Toughness Test," *New York Times*, November 3, 1985, n.d, http://query.nytimes.com/gst/fullpage.html?res=9A0CE4D61438F930A35752C1A963948260 (November 9, 2006).

37 CNN, "Then and Now: Geraldine Ferraro," *CNN*, June 19, 2005, n.d., http://www.cnn.com/2005/US/02/13/ccn25.tan.ferraro/index.html (November 9, 2006).

37 Dowd, "Toughness Test."

37 *Time*, "A Credible Candidacy and Then Some."

38 Sherrie A. Inness, ed., *Disco Divas: Women and Popular Culture in the 1970s* (Philadelphia: University of Pennsylvania Press, 2003), 3.

39 Jane Wilson, "Hollywood Flirts with the New Woman," *New York Times*, May 27, 1977, Arts and Leisure, 47.

42 Judy Klemesrud, "Feminists Recoil at Film Designed to Relate to Them," *New York Times*, February 26, 1975, n.d., http://select.nytimes.com/gst/abstract.html?res=F00E13F63559157493C4AB1789D85F418785F9 (November 9, 2006).

42 Ibid.

42 Ibid.

45 Whitney Womack, "Reevaluating 'Jiggle TV,'" *Disco Divas: Women and Popular Culture in the 1970s* (Philadelphia: University of Pennsylvania Press, 2003), 151.

46 *Time*, "TV's Super Women," November 22, 1976, n.d., http://www.time.com/time/magazine/article/0,9171,914689,00.html (February 7, 2007).

46 *Time*, Letters, December 13, 1976, n.d., http://www.time.com/time/magazine/printout/0,8816,918519,00.html (November 9, 2006).

46 *Time*, "Those Liberated Angels," November 6, 2000, n.d., http://www.time.com/time/magazine/article/0,9171,998426,00.html (November 9, 2006).

47 "Policewomen: How Well Are They Doing a "Man's" Job?" Ladies Home Journal (April 1975) 124.

47 Ibid., 82

47 Polly Home, "A Comparison of the Attitudes of Male Police Officers toward Female Police Officers from 1976 to 1994," *Florida Department of Law Enforcement*, n.d., http://www.fdle.state.fl.us/FCJEI/SLP%20papers/Horne2%20.pdf (February 7, 2007).

48 *Time*, "How Bobby Runs and Talks, Talks, Talks," November 20, 1973, n.d., http://www.time.com/time/magazine/article/0,9171,907843,00.html (November 9, 2006).

48 Bart Barnes, "Tennis Star Bobby Riggs Dies," *Washington Post*, October 27, 1995. 1995, http://www.washingtonpost.com/wp-srv/sports/longterm/memories/1995/95pass5.htm (June 15, 2007).

49 Billie Jean King, "Commencement Address," *University of Massachusetts Commencement*, May 21, 2000, http://www.umass.edu/commencement/2000/sounds/kingtranscript.pdf (February 7, 2007).

49 Ibid.

49 Larry Schwartz, "Billie Jean Won for All Women," *ESPN.com*, n.d., http://espn.go.com/sportscentury/features/00016060.html (February 7, 2007).

50 Ibid.

51 Sally K. Ride, University of California, n.d. http://casswww.ucsd.edu/personal/sride.html (June 17, 2007)

51 *Time*, "Sally's Joy Ride into the Sky," June 13, 1983, n.d., http://www.time.com/time/magazine/article/0,9171,952021,00.html (November 9, 2006).

51 Ibid.

51 Ibid.

53 Stephanie Nolen, *Promised the Moon: The Untold Story of the First Women in the Space Race* (New York: Four Walls Eight Windows, 2002), 306.

53 Ibid.

53 *Time*, "Mission Accomplished," July 4, 1983, n.d., http://www.time.com/time/magazine/article/0,9171,950918,00.html (November 9, 2006).

56 Peter Kerr, "Women in Take-Charge Roles Stride into TV's Limelight," *New York Times*, September 16, 1984, n.d., http://select.nytimes.com/search/restricted/article?res=F20F10F63B5C0C758DDDA00894DC484D81 (November 11, 2006).

57 Ibid.

58 Robert Lindsey, "Stewardesses Fight Weight Rule," *New York Times*, March 4, 1972, 29.

59 Mary Kay Bentley, "The Body of Evidence," in Sharon R. Mazzarella and Norma Odom Pecora, eds., *Growing Up Girls: Popular Culture and the Construction of Identity* (New York; Peter Lang, 1999), 209–210.

60 Ibid., 210.

60 Ibid.

61 Naomi Wolf, *The Beauty Myth, How Images of Beauty Are Used Against Women* (New York: Harper Perennial, 2002), 82.

61 Ibid., 84.

63 Ibid., 185.

63 Kilbourne, *Can't Buy Me Love: How Advertising Changes the Way We Think and Feel* (New York: Touchstone, 1999), 133.

65 Dava Sobel, "The Science of Dieting," *New York Times*, February 24, 1981, n.d., http://query.nytimes.com/gst/fullpage.html?sec=health&res=9F0DE6D81439F937A15751C0A967948260 (November 9, 2006).

66 Barrett, Stephen, "Cellulite Removers," *Nutrition Forum*, September 1999, n.d., http://findarticles.com/p/articles/mi_m0GCU/is_5_16/ai_56881797 (March 20, 2007).

68 *Time*, "Battle of the Bulges," March 1, 1975, n.d., http://www.time.com/time/magazine/article/0,9171,917209,00.html (December 11, 2007).

69 Nina Darnton, "Battle of the Bulges," *Newsweek*, March 2, 1992, 370.

69 Ibid.

69 Kilbourne, *Can't Buy Me Love*, 135.

69 Jean Seligmann, "Let Them Eat Cake," *Newsweek*, August 17, 1992, 57.

71 Wolf, *Beauty Myth*, 264.

71 Jane R. Hirschmann and Carol H. Munter, *Overcoming Overeating* (New York: Ballantine Books, 1989), 11.

72 Carol H. Munter and Jane R. Hirschmann, "The Long and Winding Road," *Overcoming Overeating Newsletter*, June 1995, n.d., http://www.overcomingovereating.com/June95.html (February 7, 2007).

73 Sarah Weddington, *A Question of Choice* (New York: Penguin, 1992), 52.

75 Ibid., 132.

75 Ibid.

78 Laura M. Carpenter, "From Girls into Women: Scripts for Sexuality and Romance: *Seventeen* Magazine, 1974–1994," *Journal of Sex Research*, May 1998, n.d., http://www.findarticles.com/p/articles/mi_m2372/is_n2_v35/ai_20846993/pg_3 (March 20, 2007).

79 Shawn Adams, Ana Garner, and Helen M. Sterk, "Narrative: Analysis of Sexual Etiquette in Teenage Magazines," *Journal of Communication*, 48 (1998): 67–69.

80 Elizabeth Larsen, "Censoring Sex Information: The Story of "Sassy," *Utne Reader*, July 1990, 96–97.

80 Ibid.

81 Rickey Wright, "Commercial Calls for Girls to Play Sports," *Virginian-Pilot*, September 22, 1995, n.d., http://scholar.lib.vt.edu/VA-news/VA-Pilot/issues/1995/vp950922/09220071.htm (November 10, 2006).

82 Ibid.

84 Barbara Huebner, "Rowers Find a Hero: Yale Protest Made Splash in Title IX," *Boston Globe*, October 21, 1999, E1.

84 Julie Wolf, "Water Fight, a Review of 'A Hero for Daisy,' " February 2000, n.d., http://www.newenglandfilm.com/news/archives/00february/hero.htm (November 9, 2006).

90 "Madonna and Her Clones," *New York Times*, n.d. http://select.nytimes.com/search/restricted/article?res=FB0D1FFB3E5D0C748CDDAF0894DD484D81 (June 16, 2007

90 Jay Cocks, "These Big Girls Don't Cry," *Time*, May 4, 1985, n.d., http://www.time.com/time/magazine/printout/0,8816,961982,00.html (November 9, 2006).

90 Peter Jennings and Todd Brewster, *The Century* (New York: Doubleday, 1998), 480.

91 Bill Dow, "Getting Beyond Mr. Mom: Confessions of a Stay-at-Home Dad," *Metro Parent Magazine*, February 1999, available online at *slowlane.com*, n.d., http://www.slowlane.com/articles/media/gettingbeyondmrmom.html (February 8, 2007).

92 William E. Pemberton, *Exit with Honor* (Armond, NY: M. E. Sharpe, Inc., 1998), 123.

93 Albin Krebs and Robert McG. Thomas Jr., "Notes on People; Explaining China," *New York Times*, October 9, 1981, http://select.nytimes.com/search/restricted/article?res=F10E17FA395D0C7A8CDDA90994D9484D81 (November 10, 2006).

93 E. Grayton Carter, "People," *Time*, October 26, 1981, n.d., http://jcgi.pathfinder.com/time/magazine/printout/0,8816,925016,00.html (November 15, 2006).

93 Lynn Rosellini, "First Lady Tells Critics 'I'm Just Being Myself,'" *New York Times*, October 13, 1981, http://select.nytimes.com/search/restricted/article?res=F10B11F6395D0C708DDDA90994D9484D81 (December 1, 2006).

93–94 Ibid.

94 *New York Times*, Letters, January 28, 1991, http://query.nytimes.com/gst/fullpage.html?res=9403E6DD123BF93BA15752C0A967948260 (November 10, 2006).

95 John M. Crewdson, "Nominee for High Court: A Record Defying Labels, *New York Times*, July 12, 1981, n.d., http://select.nytimes.com/search/restricted/article?res=FB0717FF345C0C718DDDAE0894D9484D81 (November 9, 2006).

95 Ed Magnuson, "The Brethren's First Sister," *Time*, July 20, 1981, n.d., http://www.time.com/time/magazine/article/0,9171,954833,00.html (November 10, 2006).

95 Ibid.

95 Ibid.

96 Jane O'Reilly, "Here Comes La Judge," *Time*, September 21, 1981, http://www.time.com/time/searchresults?query=%E2%80%9CHere+Comes+La+Judge%22 (February 1, 2007).

100 "Macy's: The Benediction," *A. M. Rousseau Photography Webpage*, n.d. htttp://www.amrousseau.com/benediction.html (June 5, 2007).

102 David LaGesse, "Heeding Her Own Voice," *U.S. News and World Report*, October 31, 2005, n.d., http://www.usnews.com/usnews/news/articles/051031/31winfrey.htm (November 9, 2006).

102 Pat Colander, "Oprah Winfrey's Odyssey. Talk-Show Host to Mogul," *New York Times*, March 12, 1989, 31.

103 Thomas Palmer, "'Reach for the Stars,' Was McAuliffe's Theme for Her Historical Space Missions," *Boston Globe*, January 29, 1986, n.d., http://www.boston.com/news/packages/shuttle/challenger_archive_mcauliffe.htm (September 1, 2006).

103 Colin Burgess, *Teacher in Space: Christa McAuliffe and the Challenger Legacy* (Omaha: University of Nebraska Press, 2000), 73.

104–105 LaGesse, "Heeding Voice."

105 Christopher Goodwin, "Americans Just Can't Get Enough of Oprah—Out Now on Newsstands," *Sunday Herald* (Glasgow), February 4, 2001, n.d., http://www.findarticles.com/p/articles/mi_qn4156/is_20010204/ain13956063 (November 9, 2006).

106 Guerrilla Girls, *Bitches, Bimbos, and Ballbreakers: The Guerrilla Girls' Illustrated Guide to Female Stereotypes* (New York: Penguin, 2003), 7.

109 Guerrilla Girls, *Confessions of the Guerrilla Girls* (New York: Harper Perennial, 1995), 16.

113 "Vietnam Veterans Memorial," National Park Service, May 31, 2005, http://www.nps.gov/archive/vive/memorial/servicemen.htm (June 15, 2007).

113 Linton Weeks, "Maya Lin's 'Clear Vision,'" *Washington Post*, October 20, 1995.

114 Jonathan Coleman, "First," *Time*, November 6, 1989, n.d., http://www.time.com/time/magazine/article/0,9171,958945,00.html (February 7, 2007).

114 Wolf Von Eckardt, "Storm over a Viet Nam Memorial," November 9, 1981, n.d., http://www.time.com/time/printout/0,8816,922673,00.html (February 7, 2007).

115 Margaret Carlson, "Hillary Clinton: Partner As Much As Wife," Time, n.d., http://www.time.com/time/printout/0,8816,974745,00.html (June 20, 2007).

115 JoAnn Bren Guernsey, *Hillary Rodham Clinton* (Minneapolis: Twenty-First Century Books, 2005), 59.

116 Ibid.

116 Hillary Rodham Clinton, *Living History* (New York: Simon and Schuster, 2003), 109–110.

116 Michael Kramer, "The Political Interest: How the Chicken Got Loose," *Time*, April 20, 1992, n.d., http://www.time.com/time/magazine/article/0,9171 ,975347,00.html (February 7, 2007).

116 Clinton, *Living History*, 106.

117 Ibid., 141.

117 Maureen Dowd, "The 1992 Campaign: Candidate's Wife; Hillary Clinton as Aspiring First Lady: Role Model, or a 'Hall Monitor' Type?" *New York Times*, May 18, 1992, n.d., http://select.nytimes.com/search/restricted/article ?res=F10617FB34590C7B8DDDAC0894DA494D81 (November 9, 2006).

117 Ibid.

117 Clinton, *Living History*, 110.

118 Zia Jaffrey, "Toni Morrison," *Salon*, February 2, 1998, n.d., http://www.salon.com/books/int/1998/02/cov_si _02int.html (February 7, 2007).

118 Henry Louis Gates Jr. and K. A. Appiah, *Toni Morrison: Critical Perspectives Past and Present* (New York: Amistad, 1993), 409, 408.

118 "Nobel Prize in Literature a 'Knowout' for Morrison," *Jet*, October 25, 1993, http://findarticles.com/p/articles/mi _m1355/is_n26_v84/ai_14488762 (June 14, 2007).

119–120 Dan Quayle, "Address to the Commonwealth Club of California," *Dan Quayle*, May 19, 1992, n.d., http://www.vicepresidentdanquayle.com/ speeches_StandingFirm_CCC_1.html (February 7, 2007).

123 Regina Barreca, "Leading with the Funny Bone: Humor, Gender, and the Workplace," *Harvard Management Update*, May 2001, August 6, 2001, http://hbswk.hbs.edu/archive/2403.html (March 20, 2007).

123 Joseph Boskin, *Rebellious Laughter: People's Humor in American Culture* (Syracuse, NY: Syracuse University Press, 1997), 167.

121 Susan Bolotin, "Book of the Times," *New York Times*, January 12, 1982, n.d., http://query.nytimes.com/gst/ fullpage.html?res=9507E0D71038F931A25752C0A964948 260 (November 10, 2006).

124 Anita Hill, "Opening Statement: Sexual Harassment Hearings Concerning Judge Clarence Thomas," October 11, 1991. n.d. http://www.people.virginia.edu/~ybf2u/ Thomas-Hill/1011a03.html (June 15, 2007).

124 Katherine Boo, "Universal Soldier: What Paula Coughlin Can Teach American Women," *Washington Monthly*, September 1992, n.d., http://www.findarticles.com/p/ articles/mi_m1316/is_n9_v24/ai_12530386 (March 20, 2007).

125 Eric Schmitt, "The Military Has a Lot to Learn about Women," *New York Times*, August 2, 1992, n.d., http://www.nytimes.com/books/97/06/15/reviews/ military-tailhook.html (February 7, 2007).

126 Susan Faludi, "Going Wild?" *Frontline*, 1994, http://www.pbs.org/wgbh/pages/frontline/shows/navy/ tailhook/debate.html#wild (November 9, 2006).

126 Ibid.

128 *New York Times*, "Excerpts from Supreme Court Ruling on Sexual Harassment in Workplace," November 10, 1993.

128 Andrea Sachs, "9-Zip! I Love It!" *Time*, November 22, 1993, n.d., http://www.time.com/time/magazine/ article/0,9171,979608,00.html (November 15, 2006).

130 Mark Starr and Martha Brant, "It Went Down to the Wire," *Newsweek*, July 19, 1999, 46.

131 Rick Reilly, "The Goal-Goal Girls," *Sports Illustrated*, July 6, 1999, n.d., http://sportsillustrated.cnn.com/ inside_game/magazine/lifeofreilly/1999/0705/ (November 14, 2006).

131 *Newsweek*, Letters, August 9, 1999, 15.

132 Margaret Carlson, "Why It Was More Than a Game," *Time*, July 19, 1999, n.d., http://www.time.com/time/ magazine/article/0,9171,991544,00.html (December 12, 2006).

132 *Newsweek*, "It's a GOOAAALLLL!!!!" August 9, 1999, 15.

132 Ibid.

132 *Time*, Letters, July 17, 1999, n.d., http://www.time.com/ time/magazine/article/0,9171,991702,00.html (November 10, 2006).

Selected Bibliography

Allen, Martha. *The Development of Communication Networks among Women, 1963–1983*. Washington, DC: Women's Institute for Freedom of the Press, 1988. Available online at WIFP. http://www.wifp.org/homef2.html (March 20, 2007).

Bailey, Beth L. *From Front Porch to Back Seat: Courtship in Twentieth-Century America*. Baltimore: Johns Hopkins University Press, 1989.

Barreca, Regina. *They Used to Call Me Snow White . . . But I Drifted*. New York: Penguin Books, 1991.

Benz, Dorothee. "The Media Factor behind the 'Hillary Factor.'" Extra! October–November 1992. Available online at *Fairness & Accuracy in Reporting* (FAIR). N.d. http://www.fair.org/index.php?page=1206 (February 7, 2007).

Boo, Katherine. "Universal Soldier: What Paula Coughlin Can Teach American Women." *Washington Monthly*, September 1992. N.d. http://www.findarticles.com/p/articles/mi_m1316/is_n9_v24/ai_12530386 (March 20, 2007).

Bradley, Patricia. *Mass Media and the Shaping of American Feminism, 1963–1975*. Jackson: University Press of Mississippi, 2003.

Brumberg, Joan Jacobs. *The Body Project: An Intimate History of American Girls*. New York: Random House, 1997.

Burgess, Colin. *Teacher in Space: Christa McAuliffe and the Challenger Legacy*. Omaha: University of Nebraska Press, 2000.

Chisholm, Shirley. "Equal Rights for Women." Speech. House of Representatives. May 21, 1969. Available online at *Special Collections Library, Duke University*. N.d. http://scriptorium.lib.duke.edu/wlm/equal/ (February 12, 2007).

Cho, Emily. *Looking, Working, Living Terrific 24 Hours a Day: Get Your Life in Order with Personal Style*. New York: G. P. Putnam's Sons, 1982.

Clinton, Hillary Rodham. *Living History*. New York: Simon and Schuster, 2003.

Congress, House, Committee on Education and Labor. *Discrimination Against Women*. Testimony of Pauli Murray. Committee on Education and Labor. 91st Congress, 2nd Session. Washington, DC: U.S. Government Printing Office, 1970. Available online at *History Matters*. N.d. http://historymatters.gmu.edu/d/6472 (February 7, 2007).

Douglas, Susan. *Where the Girls Are: Growing Up Female with the Mass Media*. New York: Random House, 1994.

Douglas, Susan, and Meredith W. Michaels. *The Mommy Myth: The Idealization of Motherhood and How It Has Undermined All Women*. New York; Free Press, 2004.

Dow, Bonnie J. *Prime-Time Feminism: Television, Media Culture, and the Women's Movement Since 1970*. Philadelphia: University of Pennsylvania Press, 1996.

———. "Spectacle, Spectatorship, and Gender Anxiety in Television News Coverage of the 1970 Women's Strike for Equality." *Communication Studies*, Summer 1999, n.d. http://findarticles.com/p/articles/mi_qa3669/is_199907/ai_n8830117 (June 8, 2007).

Ehrenreich, Barbara, and Deirdre English. *For Her Own Good: Two Centuries of the Experts' Advice to Women*. New York: Anchor Books, 2005.

Evans, Sara M. *Tidal Wave: How Women Changed America at Century's End*. New York: Free Press, 2003.

Faludi, Susan. Backlash: *The Undeclared War against American Women*. New York: Anchor Books, 1991.

Farrell, Amt Erdman. *Yours in Sisterhood: Ms. Magazine and the Promise of Popular Feminism*. Chapel Hill: University of North Carolina Press, 1998.

Friedan, Betty. *The Feminine Mystique*. New York: W. W. Norton, 1997.

Gaglia, Amy. "Homeless Women," An Annotated Bibliography Prepared for the Institute for the Study of Homelessness and Poverty at the Weingart Center and the California Women's Law Center, Los Angeles, February 1999.

Gates, Henry Louis, Jr., and K. A. Appiah. *Toni Morrison: Critical Perspectives Past and Present*. New York: Amistad, 1993.

Giddings, Paul. "Fighting Jane Crow." *The Nation*, May 23, 1987, 689–690.

Grimes, William. "Toni Morrison Is '93 Winner of Nobel Prize in Literature," *New York Times*, October 8, 1993.

Guernsey, JoAnn Bren. *Hillary Rodham Clinton*. Minneapolis: Twenty-First Century Books, 2005.

Halper, Donna L. *Invisible Stars: A Social History of Women in American Broadcasting.* Armonk, NY: M. E. Sharpe, 2001.

Haynes, Johnson. *The Best of Times: America in the Clinton Years.* New York: Harcourt, 2001.

Hirschmann, Jane R., and Carol H. Munter. *Overcoming Overeating.* New York: Ballantine Books, 1989.

Home, Polly. "A Comparison of the Attitudes of Male Police Officers toward Female Police Officers from 1976 to 1994." *Florida Department of Law Enforcement.* N.d. http://www.fdle.state.fl.us/fcjei (February 7, 2007).

Inness, Sherrie A., ed. *Disco Divas: Women and Popular Culture in the 1970s.* Philadelphia: University of Pennsylvania Press, 2003.

Israel, Betsy. *Bachelor Girl: 100 Years of Breaking the Rules—a Social History of Living Single.* New York: Perennial, 2002.

Johnson, Nicholas. *Test Pattern for Living.* New York: Bantam Books, 1972.

Kellner, Douglas. *Media Culture: Cultural Studies, Identity, and Politics between the Modern and the Postmodern.* New York: Routledge, 1995.

Kerber, Linda K., and Jane Sherron De Hart, eds. *Women's America: Refocusing the Past.* 4th ed. New York: Oxford University Press, 1995.

Kilbourne, Jean. *Can't Buy Me Love: How Advertising Changes the Way We Think and Feel.* New York: Touchstone, 1999.

Linsalata, Phil. "Nike's Latest Campaign Targets Self-Esteem." *Milwaukee Journal Sentinel,* September 24, 1995.

Lipton, Joshua. "She Took Her Own Route," *Columbia Journalism Review,* November–December 2001, http://findarticles.com/p/articles/mi_qa3613/is_200111/ai_n8993366 (June 8, 2007).

Lustig, Suzanne. "How and Why Did the Guerrilla Girls Alter the Art World Establishment in New York City, 1985–1995?" *State University of New York at Binghamton.* April 1, 2004. http://womhist.binghamton.edu/ggirls/intro.htm (February 8, 2007).

Malkin, Amy R. "Women and Weight: Gendered Messages on Magazine Covers." *Sex Roles: A Journal of Research,* April 1999, 647–645.

Mazzarella, Sharon R., and Norma Odom Pecora, eds. *Growing Up Girls: Popular Culture and the Construction of Identity.* New York: Peter Lang, 1999.

Molloy, John T. *Dress for Success.* New York: Peter H. Wyden, 1975.

New York Times. "Excerpts from Supreme Court Ruling on Sexual Harassment in Workplace," November 10, 1993.

Nobel Prize. "Nobel Prize in Literature 1993." *Nobelprize.org.* N.d. http://search.nobelprize.org/search/nobel/?q=toni+morrison&i=en (February 7, 2007).

Nolen, Stephanie. *Promised the Moon: The Untold Story of the First Women in the Space Race.* New York: Four Walls Eight Windows, 2002.

O'Neill, Molly. "A Growing Movement Fights Diets Instead of Fat." *New York Times,* April 12, 1992.

Peril, Lynn. *Pink Think: Becoming a Woman in Many Uneasy Lessons.* New York: W. W. Norton, 2002.

Pogrebin, Letty Cottin. "The Working Woman: Husbands Talk about Working Wives," *Ladies' Home Journal,* March 1975, 66, 69 128.

Raymond, Diane, ed. *Sexual Politics and Popular Culture.* Bowling Green, OH: Bowling Green State University Popular Press, 1990.

Riordan, Teresa. *Inventing Beauty.* New York: Broadway Books, 2004.

Rodnitzky, Jerry L. *Feminist Phoenix: The Rise and Fall of a Feminist Counterculture.* New York: Praeger, 1999.

Schlafly, Phyllis. "The Thoughts of One Who Loves Life as a Woman . . ." In Linda K. Kerber and Jane Sherron De Hart. *Women's America: Refocusing the Past.* 4th ed. New York: Oxford University Press, 1995.

Schwartz, Larry. "Billie Jean Won for All Women." *ESPN.com.* N.d. http://espn.go.com/sportscentury/features/00016060.html (February 7, 2007).

Scott, Linda. *Fresh Lipstick: Redressing Fashion and Feminism.* New York: Palgrave Macmillan, 1994.

Sports Illustrated, "The Goal-Goal Girls!" July 5, 1999. http://sportsillustrated.cnn.com/inside_game/magazine/lifeofreilly/1999/0705/ (November 14, 2006).

Tolman, Lynne. "WWII Woman Pilots Gather, Toast 1st U.S. Female Astronaut." *Boston Globe,* June 19, 1983.

Weddington, Sarah. *A Question of Choice.* New York: Penguin, 1992.

Weeks, Linton. "May Lin's 'Clear Vision.'" *Washington Post,* October 20, 1995.

Wolf, Naomi. *The Beauty Myth: How Images of Beauty Are Used Against Women.* New York: Harper Perennial, 2002.

Further Reading and Websites

BOOKS

Bartimus, Tad, Denby Fawcett, Jurate Kazickas, Edith Lederer, Ann Bryan Mariano, Anne Morrissy Merick, Laura Palmer, Kate Webb, and Tracy Wood. *War Torn: Stories of War from the Women Reporters Who Covered Vietnam.* New York: Random House, 2002.

Briggs, Carole S. *Women in Space.* Minneapolis: Twenty-First Century Books, 1999.

Frost, Shelley, and Ann Troussieux. *Throw Like a Girl: Discovering the Body, Mind and Spirit of the Athlete in You.* Hillsboro, OR: Beyond Words Publishing, 2000.

Gurnsey, JoAnn Bren. *Hillary Rodham Clinton.* Minneapolis: Twenty-First Century Books, 2005.

Joyner-Kersee, Jackie. *A Kind of Grace: The Autobiography of the World's Greatest Female Athlete.* New York: Warner Books, 1997.

Jukes, Mavis, Lilian Wai-Hin Cheung, and Debra Ziss. *Be Healthy, It's a Girl Thing: Food, Fitness and Feeling Great.* New York: Crown Publishers, 2003.

Krohn, Katherine. *Oprah Winfrey.* Minneapolis: Twenty-First Century Books, 2002.

Lanin, Joanne. *Billie Jean King: Tennis Trailblazer.* Minneapolis: Twenty-First Century Books, 1999.

Levy, Debbie. *The Vietnam War.* Minneapolis: Twenty-First Century Books, 2004.

Miller, Brandon Marie. *Dressed for the Occasion: What Americans Wore 1620–1970.* Minneapolis: Twenty-First Century Books, 1999.

Zeinert, Karen. *The Valiant Women of the Vietnam War.* Minneapolis: Twenty-First Century Books, 2000.

WEBSITES

Advertising

Advertising Council Archives.
http://web.library.uiuc.edu/ahx/advert.htm
Established in 1986, the Advertising Council Archives at the University of Illinois houses sixty years of documents created by the Ad Council since its inception in 1942. The archives contain not only the advertisements themselves—including print, radio, and television—but also documents that tell the stories behind the campaigns.

TV Party.
http://www.tvparty.com
This site provides access to television shows and commercials from the 1950s to the 1980s.

Film

MacDonald & Associates.
http://www.macfilms.com
This site provides a historical film archive of the twentieth century. Topics include politics, medicine, sports, family life, travel, newsreels, animated cartoons, musical performance, and war as seen through the lens of the motion picture camera.

Society and Social Customs

Guerrilla Girls.
http://www.guerrillagirls.com
This site provides provocative text, visuals, and humor related to feminism, discrimination, and social change.

National Museum of American History.
http://americanhistory.si.edu/collections
This site provides a searchable database of exhibitions covering many of the topics touched upon in this book, including fashions, working women, and war posters. The site includes oral histories, prints, photographs, and drawings.

Women's Issues

The National Organization for Women.
http://www.now.org/index.html
NOW is the largest organization of feminist activists in the United States. This website provides news articles and updates on a wide range of issues affecting women, including family, child care, Title IX, and women in the military.

U.S. Department of Labor, Women's Bureau.
http://www.dol.gov/wb
The Women's Bureau is a valuable source of information about employment-related initiatives specific to women workers and business owners. It provides up-to-date news on wages and workplace safety as well as various fields of employment.

Index

About the Author

Catherine Gourley is an award-winning author and editor of books for young adults. A former editor of *Read* magazine, Gourley is the national director for Letters About Literature, a reading-writing promotion program of the Center for the Book in the Library of Congress. In addition, she is the curriculum writer for the Story of Moves, an educational outreach program on film study and visual literacy in the middle school developed by the Film Foundation, Los Angeles.

Among Gourley's more than twenty books are *Media Wizards* and *Society's Sisters* as well as the other four volumes in the Images and Issues of Women in the Twentieth Century series—*Gibson Girls and Suffragists: Perceptions of Women from 1900 to 1918, Flappers and the New American Woman: Perceptions of Women from 1918 through the 1920s, Rosie and Mrs. America: Perceptions of Women in the 1930s and 1940s,* and *Gidgets and Women Warriors: Perceptions of Women in the 1950s and 1960s.*

Photo Acknowledgments

The images in this book are used with the permission of: Library of Congress, pp. 3, 9, 12, 18 (both), 21, 30; © Bettmann/CORBIS, pp. 4, 16, 73 (right), 93, 112; © JP Laffont/Sygma/CORBIS, pp. 6, 11 (left), 13, 32; Private Collection, pp. 7, 27 (top left), 28, 62, 63, 64, 74, 77, 79 (all), 81; Diana Davies Collection, Manuscripts and Archives Division, The New York Public Library, Astor, Lenox and Tilden Foundations, p. 11 (right); © Yale Joel/Time Life Pictures/Getty Images, p. 14; © Don Hogan Charles/Hulton Archive/Getty Images, p. 15; Image courtesy of The Advertising Archives, pp. 19, 27 (top right and bottom right); © Ankers Capitol Photographers, p. 20; "Book Cover", copyright © 1970, from SISTERHOOD IS POWERFUL by Robin Morgan. Used by permission of Random House, Inc., p. 22; Reprinted by permission of *Ms.* magazine, © 1972, p. 23; Reprinted by permission of *Ms.* magazine, © 1973, Image courtesy of The Advertising Archives, p. 24 (left); Photograph by Richard Avedon. Courtesy of *VOGUE*, Condé Nast Publications Inc., p. 24 (right); © Cynthia Macadams/ Time Life Pictures/Getty Images, p. 25; © Terry O'Neill/Hulton Archive/Getty Images, p. 26; © Michael Mauney/Time Life Pictures/Getty Images, p. 29; © Hulton Archive/Getty Images, pp. 34, 35, 43, 46, 59; © Roger Ressmeyer/CORBIS, pp. 36, 80; Everett Collection, pp. 38, 39, 41, 44, 48, 56; © Ted Streshinsky/CORBIS, p. 47; NASA, pp. 51, 52, 103; © Ray Fisher/Time Life Pictures/Getty Images, p. 54; © CBS/Landov, pp. 55, 101; Courtesy of Universal Studios Licensing, LLLP, Image provided by Everett Collection, p. 57; © Henry Diltz/CORBIS, p. 58; © Daryl Cagle; http://www.cagle.com/ art, p. 60; © Rose Hartman/Time Life Pictures/Getty Images, p. 61; © CBS Photo Archive/Hulton Archive/Getty Images, p. 65; AP Photo, p. 67; U.S. Food and Drug Administration, p. 68; "Front Cover" by Andrew Newman, copyright © 1998 by Andrew Newman (Cover Design), Cover photograph © 1998 by Abigail Huller, from IT'S NOT ABOUT FOOD by Carol Emery Normandi and Laurelee Roark. Used by permission of G. P. Putnam's Sons, a division of Penguin Group (USA) Inc., p. 69; © Kirk Condyles/The Image Works, p. 70; © Martha Holmes/Time Life Pictures/Getty Images, p. 71; © Diana Walker/Time Life Pictures/Getty Images, p. 73 (left); © Taro Yamasaki/Time Life Pictures/Getty Images, p. 75; Used with permission from Planned Parenthood® Federation of America, Inc. © 2007 PPFA. All rights reserved. Image courtesy of The Advertising Archives, p. 76 (left); Kruger, Barbara, Untitled (your body is a battleground), 1989, photographic silkscreen on vinyl, 112x112 inches, The Broad Art Foundation, Santa Monica. Courtesy: Mary Boone Gallery, New York. Image courtesy of The Advertising Archives, p. 76 (right); Photo from the film, A HERO FOR DAISY (www.aherofordaisy.com). Courtesy of Mary Mazzio and 50 Eggs Films. © 1999 50 Eggs LLC., p. 84; Copyright © 1976 Yale Daily News Publishing Company, Inc. All rights reserved. Reprinted with permission, p. 85; © Brian Bahr/Allsport/ Getty Images, p. 86; AP Photo/Michael Schmelling, p. 87; © Neal Preston/CORBIS, p. 88; © David McGough/Time Life Pictures/Getty Images, p. 89; © 1983, MGM. All rights reserved. Courtesy of MGM CLIP + STILL, Image provided by Everett Collection, p. 91; The White House, pp. 92, 117; © Keystone/Consolidated News Pictures/Getty Images, p. 96; © Viviane Moos/CORBIS, p. 98; © Ann Marie Rousseau, p. 100; © Star File, Inc., p. 104; Courtesy www.guerillagirls.com, pp. 106, 107; Copyright © 1989 Guerrilla Girls, Courtesy www.guerillagirls.com, p. 109; Copyright © 1992 Guerrilla Girls, Courtesy www.guerillagirls.com, p. 110; Copyright © 1995 Guerrilla Girls, Courtesy www.guerillagirls.com, p. 111; © Wally McNamee/CORBIS, p. 113; Arkansas Democrat-Gazette, p. 115; © AFP/Getty Images, pp. 118, 130; MURPHY BROWN © Warner Bros. Inc. All Rights Reserved. Image provided by Everett Collection, p. 120; © Brad Markel/Liaison/Getty Images, p. 122; © USAF/Getty Images, p. 125; © J. GURZINSKI/CORBIS SYGMA, p. 126; © Fritz Hoffmann/Image Works/Time Life Pictures/Getty Images, p. 128.

Front Cover: © Evelyn Floret/Time Life Pictures/Getty Images (front); © Susan Aimee Weinik/Time Life Pictures/Getty Images (background).